ROBBIE WILLIAMS
SOMEBODY SOMEDAY

ROBBIE WILLIAMS
SOMEBODY SOMEDAY

Words by Mark McCrum
Photos by Scarlet Page

EBURY
PRESS

'Inside my tour, my head and my pants…'

www.robbiewilliams.com

First published in Great Britain in 2001

This edition published in Great Britain in 2002

10 9 8 7 6 5 4 3 2

Text © Robert Williams and Mark McCrum

Photographs © Scarlet Page

Robert Williams and Mark McCrum have asserted their right to be identified as the
authors of this work under the Copyright, Designs and Patents Act 1988.

First published by
Ebury Press
Random House
20 Vauxhall Bridge Road
London SW1 2SA

Random House Australia (Pty) Limited
20 Alfred Street, Milsons Point
Sydney
New South Wales 2061
Australia

Random House New Zealand Limited
18 Poland Road, Glenfield,
Auckland 10
New Zealand

Random House South Africa (Pty) Limited
Endulini, 5A Jubilee Road
Parktown 2193
South Africa

Random House UK Limited Reg. No. 954009

www.randomhouse.co.uk

www.markmccrum.com

A CIP catalogue record for this book is available from the British Library

ISBN 0 09 188473X

Papers used by Ebury Press are natural, recyclable products made from
wood grown in sustainable forests

Project management for IE Music: Gabby Chelmicka
Art direction and design: Push
Printed and bound by Cox & Wyman Ltd, Reading, Berks

Contents

1 We Shall See What Happens   15
2 The Stockholm Jinx   33
3 Orange Juice Rave   65
4 Robbie World   83
5 Trying to Find Robert   111
6 Rock 'n' Roll Veteran   129
7 New Rob   147
8 Rock DJ   167
9 Can You Kick It   197
10 Be Arsed!   221
11 I'm Ace   253
12 Turnaround   271
13 Swinging Westward   285

The Sermon On
The Mount Tour

Band Party

Robbie Williams	The Preacher
Guy Chambers	Musical director/producer/keyboards/guitar
Gary Nuttall	Guitar
Fil Eisler	Guitar
Yolanda Charles	Bass guitar
Chris Sharrock	Drums
Claire Worrall	Keyboards/guitar
Tessa Niles	Backing vocals
Katie Kissoon	Backing vocals
Tim Clark	Manager
David Enthoven	Manager
Josie Cliff	Management/Rob's PA
Andy 'Franksy' Franks	Tour manager
Tom Golseth	Tour accountant
Simon 'Jonah' Jones	Security
Aegon 'Marv' Welsh	Security
Jeremy Stacey	Drums
Phil Spalding	Bass
Neil Taylor	Guitar

Crew Party

Wob Roberts	Production manager
Lizzie Adshead	Production assistant
Flo Guenand	Wardrobe
Gary Currier	Stage Manager
Jez Craddick	Rigger
Liz Berry	Creative director/lighting designer
Mark England	Lighting crew chief
Barry Branford	Lighting crew
Dave Bracey	Front-of-house sound engineer
Martin Wareing	Monitor engineer
Bart Schoonbaert	Sound crew
Dave Poynter	Sound crew
Sherif El Barbari	Sound crew
Sarne Thorogood	Sound crew
Adam Birch	Guitar technician
Jules Bowen	Keyboard technician
Jez Webb	Guitar technician
Mick Winder	Drum technician
Duncan 'Pompey' Wilkinson	Security
Alastair MacDairmid	Video projection
Rick Worsfold	Head carpenter

George Osborne	Carpenter
Andy Jupp	Rigger/carpenter
Graham Morrison	Head chef
Mairead De Barra	Caterer
Em Franklin	Caterer
Chris Clarke	Caterer
Kathryn Bernie	Caterer
Richard 'Richie' Stevenson	Merchandise
Waff Walker	Merchandise
Simon Lake	Lead Truck Driver
Andy Rauax	Truck Driver
Richard Crook	Truck Driver
Julian Meynell	Truck Driver
Paul Bricusse	Truck Driver
Ian Silver	Truck Driver
John Mulholland	Band Bus Driver
Maurice Good	Band Bus Driver
Mick Birch	Crew Bus Driver
Ray Valks	Crew Bus Driver
Bobbie Smith	Crew Bus Driver

'If I'm drinking and taking drugs, I'm the last person on earth that I'd want my daughter to go out with.

But hopefully the person that I will become will be somebody I'd let my daughter go out with.'

WE SHALL SEE
WHAT HAPPENS

It's well after two o'clock on the second day of rehearsals and everyone's waiting for Rob. At one end of the vast, concrete-floored oval that is the Docklands London Arena, the set is up: the rows of lights, the stacks of speakers, the white cyclorama, the drapes, the black front curtain, all miraculously suspended from the criss-crossed girders in the roof high above. On the stage itself the instruments are laid out and ready: the drums central on their platform, the groups of keyboards to left and right, the guitars in racks beyond. On the fringes a mighty confusion of wires and plugs connect to a mass of chunky black cabinets and monitors. Smoke drifts across from two stage-side smoke machines and hangs thinly in the air, giving substance to the beams of the continually changing coloured lights in the half-darkness.

The seven members of the band have arrived, greeted each other and various black T-shirted members of the crew with elaborate hugs, wandered backstage to catering for coffee or lunch and eventually taken their places on the set. Curly-haired Guy Chambers, Rob's songwriting collaborator and the band's musical director, has settled down behind his keyboard stack and started the rehearsal. 'Is everyone ready?' he asks. Languid black bass guitarist Yolanda Charles unties her hair and they swing into it. But still the tall central microphone waits redundant on its stand, as it did throughout the long day of studio rehearsals yesterday.

Suddenly there's a cry away to the right. 'Robbie!' It is the star himself, at last, striding through the gloom in a posse of three or four, his dark-bobbed personal assistant Josie Cliff keeping in step beside him. It's quite chilly, this early February day, and he's wrapped up: in thick coat, grey woolly hat, dark glasses, a scarf wrapped tight round his neck. As he marches straight to the centre of the stage, a shiver of excitement comes over the band.

'Hello, hello, hello. Nice to see everyone,' he says, nodding round, smiling, smoking as he talks. 'What's with the hair, Gary?' he asks the pudding-bowled, sideburned guitarist on the left.

'Wish I could say it was me own,' Gary Nuttall replies, with a sheepish grin.

Rob moves now to kiss Yolanda, who smiles hugely as she embraces him. He hugs Fil Eisler, the other guitarist, tall, lean and slightly scary in a fur-collared trenchcoat, shakes hands with Guy, then waves at keyboard player Claire Worrall and drummer Chris Sharrock. He blows kisses to his two backing singers, Tessa Niles and Katie Kissoon. He's still smoking, with stylish casualness; his walk is not so much a swagger, but more the confident stride of a man surveying his domain.

'Shall we do "Wimmin"?' asks Guy, up at his keyboard set, keeping things gently moving along. 'D'you want to do "Wimmin", Rob?'

'Let's do "Wimmin",' Rob replies. 'I'm sick of blokes.'

There's a ripple of laughter across the band, crew and other hangers-on who fringe the brightly lit stage area.

As the band launch into Rob's new song, the energy is completely different. With Rob there, holding that microphone, his voice at the centre of the music, everything suddenly coheres. 'Even before he sings a note,' says Tessa later, 'his presence is enough to kick-start the thing into hyperspace.'

'Stop!' calls Rob suddenly, halfway through the song. There is silence. 'On the answer lines,' he continues commandingly, 'can they be really shouty and can everyone do 'em.' As the band listens attentively, he demonstrates: 'Nice tits, nice arse, no class or conversation.'

The band try it out, yelling back his chorus. Rob does a little thrust on the final 'Whoa!' and throws his fist up in the air. Then he's gone – off to join the tall figure of tour manager Andy 'Franksy' Franks at the far side of the stage, dressed, as always, in his habitual black. Rob wasn't on stage for long. The band are left electrified by his presence, laughing like kids.

As star follows tour manager through the little door to backstage and catering, MD Guy is quietly back in charge. The band rehearse 'Singing For The Lonely' and 'Perfect Day', but it's all a bit lacklustre again. Behind them, a wiry, bald crew member pumps up one of the two giant inflatable Brit awards that flank the back of the stage. Then, just as the band are flagging badly, Rob has sprung on from nowhere, grabbed the mike, and kicked the act back into life. 'It's such a perfect day,' he growls in a powerful, deliberately non-singing voice. 'I'm glad I spent it with you.'

He's slowly disrobing now. His coat's off (though not the woolly hat and scarf), revealing an untucked cream shirt, criss-crossed with dark lines. Below, his baggy jeans crumple over trainers.

'I'm so sick of people's expectations, leaves me tired all the time...'

Even in this empty stadium, Rob sings with such intense passion, his high forehead furrowed into a frown as he clutches the mike stand with both hands. His voice rings up to where the multicoloured lights flicker across the shadowed spaces of the roof.

'I was watching that Popstars thing on Saturday night,' he tells his ragtag audience during a break a little later. 'And I was thinking, if I auditioned for that now, I wouldn't get it.' There is laughter. 'And then,' he continues, in a spooky voice, 'I remembered...'

Halfway through 'No Regrets' he breaks off. 'We know all of these,' he says. 'So we don't need to do the rest of them.'

'I've soon got to get up
in front of thousands
of people daily.

But that's my life.

It's bonkers to think that
this person, feeling how
I feel, is going to get up
and generate 10,000
people to have a good
time.

I don't know how I'm
going to do it.'

Up behind his keyboard, Guy's face is a wry and impenetrable mask. You get the feeling that he'd like to finish the set, but he doesn't complain about this abruptly terminated rehearsal. He just wants to try Rob quickly with the new intro for 'Rock DJ', he says. So Rob turns to face his band as they play him the theme music from 2001: A Space Odyssey, which they practised earlier and for two long hours yesterday. Is he about to cancel all their hard work? But no, he nods, slowly, and gives Guy the thumbs up.

'Can I have everyone on the tour in the catering room after this?' Rob announces, as the rehearsal ends. Band and crew troop after him across the floor and down the corridor to catering. Rob sits central at a table with everyone around him, some sitting, some standing, all expectant. No-one is quite sure why they're here, but Rob's always full of surprises. Is he about to give them a novel pre-tour pep talk?

Rob looks round slowly, taking everyone in with those extraordinarily powerful eyes of his (green, when you look at them twice). 'I don't know if you're aware,' he begins. 'A few of you are, a few of you aren't. I've stopped drinking and taking drugs and so —' He breaks off with a chuckle. 'I know a lot of you have been around me before, where I've stopped drinking and taking drugs only to see me start again. Now I don't know if I'm going to keep it up this time, but I really want to,' he continues earnestly, 'I really, really want to. So I want you to know that around me, in confined spaces, when I can't leave, say, on planes, or in tour buses, it's increasingly difficult for me to see you all pissed, and to see you all do whatever you do. I'm an alcoholic and a drug addict and alcoholics and drug addicts want to drink and take drugs, even though it kills them, or upsets them, or makes your and my tour hell to be on, and I'd like never to do it again, but we shall see what happens. And that's it, basically. I love you all, I do. I feel so much love when I'm around you all. It's just a shame,' he concludes with a sudden barking cackle, 'that we have to get up on stage.'

There is loud laughter from the troops at this. Then Rob's on his feet. One of his two managers, David Enthoven, is sitting at the back of the crowd. 'Well, that was very nicely done, don't you think?' he says. Then he's off with Josie and Rob to the private car, leaving crew and band to digest this somewhat wavering declaration of intent. Rob has tried to be clean before, and failed, on numerous occasions. Is it really going to be different this time, they wonder, or is this just going to be a regular tour ritual – Rob's declaration of sobriety, which ends in a drunken and druggy collapse at some crisis moment along the way?

Spiritual Warrior
Together with partner Tim Clark, David Enthoven has been crucial in the transformation of Rob from washed-up, ex-boy-band dropout to the superstar he is today. David is a big, bald, bear of a man, with the

genial air of someone who can't quite believe his luck. When Rob first appeared in the offices of Tim and David's company, IE Music, in late 1996, just over a year after leaving Take That, he was, David remembers, 'in a bit of a sorry state'. At the time, he was being spoken of as the least likely of Take That to make it solo. Everyone in the industry was talking about Gary Barlow as the one with the talent. Enthoven admits that IE's new prospect was a bit of a punt. 'We hadn't a clue whether this was going to work,' he says. 'We had no experience of managing what I call middle-of-the-road pop, which was what Rob was at that time.'

But David had not merely liked Rob: his own earlier life (and career) having been destroyed by narcotic addiction, he also empathised with the young performer. 'Because I knew he was going through a few drinking and drugs problems. So I was able to talk to him on that level.' Now 57, he's been around the music business since the early sixties, when he left 'the most unlikely breeding ground' of Harrow to manage his first group. 'In the pop world I was classed as a posh-speaking playboy,' he admits. 'I've had my leg pulled about my accent all my life.' However unlikely his credentials, David was a rapid success, by the mid 70s managing such rock legends as King Crimson, Roxy Music, ELP and T Rex (so named because David couldn't spell Tyrannosaurus).

Soon after meeting Rob, David and Tim went over to his house to listen to demos and assess the young man's potential. 'It was all very average,' says David. 'There was probably one song in there that was reasonably interesting. Then he said, "D'you want to hear some of my poetry?" And he read that out and Tim and I just looked at each other and knew instantly that this could work. What came out of his mouth was so strong. He just painted a picture. So from that moment on I thought, Well, that's easy. All we've got to do now is find him somebody to mill that into music.'

From that day on, David has been something of a father figure for Rob. 'He's always been able to talk to me about being sober and clean and I've always encouraged that,' David says. He now accompanies Rob whenever and wherever he goes on tour. Known variously as 'Old Boy' or 'the spiritual warrior', David is totally realistic about the challenge Rob faces in trying to stay clean. 'It's not easy for a 26-year-old to grasp the nettle. I waited until I was 41. I think he knows he's had a bit of a problem for quite a long time and it's a daily battle. We've had a few stop-starts along the way – so we're not finished with that little demon.'

'Without David,' says Rob, 'I might have died. That sounds very dramatic. But this compulsion to do whatever I have to is still in me. It might return tomorrow, it might return tonight, and I might still die.'

'Guy understands me
so well and then he
completely doesn't.

I don't think he gets
my insecurities about
singing. Me thinking
I'm not much of
a singer.

He gives me enough
space to allow me to
go off and do whatever
I want and not feel
scared in his presence.'

Thou Shalt Pass

Outside the Equinox, Leicester Square, the following evening, there are no signs even mentioning the performance that Robbie Williams is scheduled to do later – for this is a private gig for Deutsche Bank (all proceeds to go to UNICEF and Robbie's charity Give It Sum which is administrated by Comic Relief) and a warm-up for the main European tour that starts this weekend. There are just a couple of crowd-control barriers, two hefty bouncers and a small gaggle of girls who've sensed that something is going on, as dressed-up people start to arrive with tickets.

If you're a member of the band, crew or Rob's immediate entourage, however, you go straight past, flashing the access-all-areas backstage pass that tour manager Franksy handed out yesterday at rehearsal. It's a shiny laminated plastic oblong, silver and green, about three inches by five, on which is written, in a suitably biblical font, 'THE SERMON ON THE MOUNT TOUR'. Below that the trademark 'RW', and then 'THOU SHALT PASS'. This will take you past a second cluster of instantly respectful heavies inside and on down the corridor to the dance floor, where you can start to smell the excitement as people gather at the downstairs bar and fill the quaint, circular-backed seats that run in a line round the front of the first-floor gallery. Here, at one side, are two hardcore Robbie fans who've managed to get in on a friend's ticket. Kelly is in her twenties and she's garrulous with enthusiasm. 'He's so brilliant. He's good-looking, he's sexy, he's so funny and normal. I just want to sleep with him and my husband's given me permission if the opportunity ever arises.'

She means it, too.

Backstage, the band have pitched up and colonised the two cramped dressing rooms marked 'MALE' and 'FEMALE'. Then Rob's arrived and is into his own dressing room with Josie and Tim and David. He's not in a great state, wan-looking and restless, as he sits in front of the make-up mirror, tapping his foot on the lino floor. He feels nervous and really empty, he's forgotten how to do it, how to entertain an audience for an hour and a half. 'Of course, I was deep in the middle of not liking myself very much then,' he will say later in the tour. Out front, the crowd by the rail is now seven deep. They're the most unlikely-looking German bankers you've ever seen – in crop tops, tight denims, glittery boob tubes. By quarter to eight, the whole dance floor is chock-a-block. The pre-show tape whips up the mood. 'This is a public announcement,' booms a voice. 'We are sorry to say that Robbie Williams will not be appearing tonight – the good news is that H from Steps will be replacing him.' Laughter and cheers. 'Robbie Williams has requested absolute silence on his entrance.' More yells. 'Robbie Williams will be on stage in one minute – tonight, he's going to be slightly effeminate – the poof!' Wild screams and wolf whistles.

Blue light flashes on the stage as the operatic 'Rob-bie! Rob-bie!' intro rings out over the din. It's one of Guy's more inspired ideas, setting the star's name to Carl Orff's famous Carmina Burana. The band run on, grinning, and take up their instruments. Over the forest of arms out front, the light goes red, white, flashing, dazzling. And here he is. Sauntering on, very cool in a dark blue pinstripe suit. 'Hello, good evening, my name is Robbie Williams. Are you ready to be entertained?'

They are. Robbie leans forward and touches one of the girls up at the rail, looking at her lingeringly as he holds her fingers. As she and her surrounding group of friends go crazy, he lets go and steps back. He takes his jacket off. Then his tie. He nods round slowly at the screaming crowd, smiling and taking them in, visibly relieved.

'You're tired of your teachers and your school's a drag, you're not going to end up like your mum and dad,' he shouts, storming into the opening 'Let Me Entertain You'. The unlikely bankers love him. By the next song, 'Lazy Days', they're singing his words back to him. He paces the front of the stage, creating little pools of excitement among the crowd.

Up on the stairs to the left of the stage are David and Tim, with PA Josie Cliff and a skinny young woman in a pale blue T-shirt – it's Geri Halliwell, no less, currently rumoured by the tabloids to be Rob's girlfriend. Josie and David bop along enthusiastically, side by side, an incongruous Little and Large pair. From time to time Robbie looks over towards his offstage supporters, registering their encouragement with a nod.

If you didn't know him, you'd never guess at what he's feeling inside. 'At that time,' he says, 'I actually had contempt for my audience for coming to see somebody so shit. I'd be on stage and I'd think What have you come to see this wanker for? It was a horrible place to be. I felt like a club singer or something.'

At the end of 'Better Man', Robbie bows and leans down over the three security guards to talk one-to-one with a bare-shouldered beauty in the front row. As he chats to her on mike, her mobile phone rings. He laughs and grabs it. 'Hi,' he says, stepping back on stage. 'It's Robbie here. What are you wearing?' Then, 'Take it off.' He's feeling a bit lonely, he adds, wondering whether the mystery caller would like to come round and sort him and about 300 other fellas out. With that wickedly simian expression, he hands back the phone. 'Bloody 'ell,' he says, 'it was 'er mum. Sorry, Mum.'

Between the songs he does this jokey stuff. Singing, he's serious. He throws his arms wide, inviting everyone in; then he crosses his hands on his heart and gives his audience a little-boy-lost look as he sings of his anger and pain. He never for a moment forgets or ignores them, and he has other ways of pulling them in: holding out the mike to get them to join in the chorus of 'She's The One'; putting his hands to his ears to encourage the (already deafening) applause after 'Supreme'; getting them to put their hands in the air for 'Millennium', so that the whole floor is a wonderful swaying forest of fingers; sitting back on the drum platform and having a drink of water while they sing 'Angels', then making them erupt when he strolls forward, applauds them and joins in to lead the chorus. 'And through it a–all, she offers me protection…'

When the show ends Rob slumps down in his dressing room backstage. Despite the rapturous reception of the crowd, his underlying mood hasn't changed. 'This is going to be a long year,' he says dejectedly to his managers.

As the audience pours happily out into Leicester Square, and a weary Rob speeds back to his flat in Notting Hill, the tiny VIP bar at the end of the gallery has become the impromptu headquarters of the IE Music team, in a state of post-gig excitement. Twenty-something Lucy Pullin is Josie Cliff's assistant and she has a cogent theory about why Rob is such a powerful performer. 'It's because of the way he interacts with the audience,' she enthuses, making evocative gestures with her wine glass. 'Notice how he held his microphone out to the audience in the middle of "No Regrets"? With that chorus line of "They tell me I'm doing fine". It's like, "Am I doing all right?" Then they roar back "yes" and that's like Rob's therapy. And that's why he's so appealing. Because they all, well, all the women, at any rate, want to heal him.' Lucy deals with all the fan letters that come into the office and even the twelve-year-olds, she reckons, are trying to say the same. 'They can't quite articulate it. They say "Don't be so sad" or something. But they all want to heal him, too.'

2

'I don't think my lifestyle is normal. It just depends again what you deem as being normal. It is normal to me. Well, no it isn't, it's totally abnormal on a day to day basis.

But I've never met anyone that's normal. They've all got their strange quirks and perversions. Or their strange ways of thinking or being.

Everybody is abnormal.'

THE STOCKHOLM JINX

Thirty-six hours later, three purpose-built crew buses and five silver equipment trucks start on the two-day road journey from King's Cross to Stockholm, taking with them production manager Wob Roberts, creative director Liz Berry, two riggers, six lighting crew ('lampeys'), six sound crew, five assorted instrument technicians, a video projection expert, three stage carpenters, a wardrobe mistress, a chef, four caterers, two merchandise salesmen, not to mention the three coach drivers, six truck drivers (one to spare), and Duncan 'Pompey' Wilkinson, the nicest security guard in the world.

A day later, Franksy gathers the other half of the equation, the sixteen-strong band party, in Heathrow's departure lounge. Standing tall in his small round black 'GB' hat and long black leather coat, he looks like a bizarre cross between a football manager and the leader of some nineteenth-century Puritan sect. Besides the musicians, there's Rob's security guys – black, shaven-headed Aegon 'Marv' Welsh and white, moustachioed Simon 'Jonah' Jones – and chubby American tour accountant Tom Golseth.

In the Club Europe business-class lounge they

settle in a loose group, reading newspapers and chatting. Franksy is showing Gary an e-mail that lists the terrible things fizzy drinks do to you; Gary's a total junk-food addict on tour, and Franksy's trying to put him back on the straight and narrow.

Claire and Yolanda sit with the two backing singers, Katie and Tessa. Yolanda laughs her infectiously dirty laugh: she sounds like Mutley from the Wacky Races and always takes a filthy joke just one step too far, hence her nickname Smutley. Claire is Champers, because no matter where they are, Yolanda says, she always manages to find a bottle of champagne. Katie Kissoon is Two Sips, because after the gigs she only ever has two sips of a drink; and Tessa is Cottonbud, because she once told the other girls a disgusting story about something you could do with a cottonbud.

Now Rob's arrived, with his immediate posse of David and Josie. He looks somehow bigger close up, with those muscled arms and striking tattoos half-visible under his T-shirt (a swirling Maori pattern on his left arm, a stern lion on his right, with 'Elvis, Grant Me Serenity' above and 'Born To Be Mild' underneath). His eyes, under those thick black brows, are hard to meet, they're so intense. He's restless, too, nodding, looking round, then suddenly concentrating for a moment on the matter in hand.

He shakes hands with or hugs his band members, then settles down to one side to play cards with David. Not poker or whist, but Uno, a kids' game where you put down your card if it's the same number or colour as the previous player's. 'It's one of those things we used to play as children,' says Josie. 'It's our game of the moment.' Rob often has compulsive fads like this: last year it was backgammon.

In the plane Rob's up in the front row of the crowded business-class section, and the cabin crew are visibly excited to have such a star on board. He's hardly shy or discreet, sitting up high in his chair, turning round to talk to Guy in the row behind, making the prettiest of the hostesses titter. David's fruity laughter and Josie's high-pitched giggles ring out above the hum of the engines. Though alcohol is of course offered, the band in the rows behind stick carefully to orange juice and mineral water.

By the time we land in Stockholm the sky is dark. It's snowing and the edge of the runway is thick with yellowing slush. As the group head down the airport corridors towards Passport Control, Rob leads the way in his tight woolly black hat and dark glasses. Security men Marv and Jonah are right beside him, eyes flicking round continually for any threat.

'There's your lovely lady,' says Fil to Gary, as a case lined with crimson silk is opened to reveal a favourite dark blue electric guitar. Rob vanishes with David, Josie and the security guys to a private car. The rest of the band watch as Franksy supervises a couple of porters pulling their cases – each piece carefully numbered with a laminated bright green tag – off the baggage reclaim belt on to a waiting trolley. Then they're out into the wintry night, where two minibuses wait by the curb. They pile in, laughing and chattering, excited to be here, abroad, at the start of their tour.

The Grand Hotel is right in the centre of Stockholm, a magnificent old building fronting on to a river where street-lit chunks of ice bob in the swirling dark current. Up by reception in the gold-carpeted lobby, Franksy hands the band members their keys and white envelopes containing a rooming list detailing their new identities. They're all booked in under false names to stop anyone getting hassled by over-zealous fans who are trying to track down Rob. When they used to go under their real names, they would be rung up at all times of day and night. 'Where is Robb-ieeeeee?'

So drummer Chris is ARTHUR BEATLATE. 'There's a reason for that,' says Fil. Fil is PHIL THEE. 'On account of his fil-thee habits,' chuckles Franksy. Gary is MUSTAFFA PEACE. Guy is JACQUES ORFF. Yolanda, for reasons she doesn't need to go into (she laughs, Smutley-style) is ANITA BUSH. Claire is JACK McGIGIN. Tessa is MISS SU MEE and Katie is SALLY VATED.

Rob crashes out in his suite with some tapes from his self-help programme. Gary paces off in search of supper. He doesn't eat junk food at home, but he doesn't much like hotel food, and anyway, he admits with his usual, self-deprecating grin, 'I'm extremely tight; they charge for bringing food up in a lift!' He'd rather save up and take his wife out to a nice restaurant when he gets back home to Englefield Green. 'Like Jack's – a lovely chippy we have.'

Having unpacked, the more gregarious members of the group gather in the bar. Guy, Claire, Fil, from the band; then Franksy the tour manager and Tom the accountant. Chris the drummer only eats out, they joke, when someone else is paying.

'Bird alert, right!' calls Claire. Three girls are approaching the group at the bar. One pretty one in a brown suede coat, and two accomplices with over-made-up eyes.

'Groupies,' says Guy, with his knowing yet almost shy smile.

Fil goes over. Look, he explains, they're all going out for some food now, but maybe later, yeah. He ushers them through into the outer bar, with its view over the glittering river. Guy is already at the door, with Franksy and the rest of the band around him.

'Don't give me your Dad look,' Claire says to Guy. The band call their MD 'the Lord', on account of his commanding ways and expensive tastes. It's not a nickname he seems to mind.

Mr Charisma
At the back of the little companion booklet to Robbie's latest album, Sing When You're Winning, is a discreet dedication: To Guy Chambers, who is as

much Robbie as I am.

'We changed one another's lives when we met,' says Guy. 'It was an instant thing. I knew immediately Rob walked into the studio and opened his mouth that he was really great. He was just this ball of energy. He had all these great lyrical ideas, and lyrics for me had always been one of my weaker points, so it was great meeting someone who could do that. I always had plenty of musical ideas, so the combination of us both was very powerful.' The second day the pair wrote 'Angels', the single that was to launch Robbie's solo career, catapulting his first album from doldrums to platinum bestseller. 'We wrote it in twenty minutes, half an hour, and when we'd finished we both realised that this was really going to work. It was – what's the word – I want to use the word 'miracle', like St Paul on the road to Damascus? It was a bit like that, meeting Rob. It was an emotional thing. It was like meeting my wife. That's the closest thing to it. Because I needed him so badly, and he really needed me so badly. When you meet someone with that mutual need thing, it's very potent.'

Until that day, 8 January 1997, Guy had been very much the struggling young musician. He was in his early 30s, playing with a band called The Lemon Trees, living in a scuzzy flat in Archway. 'My career was going nowhere,' he admits, tugging idly at his curly brown hair. 'Absolutely nowhere. I was getting quite desperate, actually. I was thinking of jacking it in and becoming a teacher. I was 32. And by that age if you haven't made it in this business, it's tough. People start thinking that's it – you're never going to make it.'

It had been a long journey to that defining moment in Guy's life. His family had always been musical: his father was a flautist with the London Philharmonic; his mother worked at Decca, and had amassed a 'huge' record collection. There was a piano in the house, and always musicians around. Someone would hammer out songs and everyone would join in: Gershwin, Elvis Presley, the hits of the day.

Guy was five when he started playing the piano, eight when he realised he could make up his own pieces and twelve when he wrote his first string quartet, shortly after he'd failed his Eleven Plus.

When Guy was thirteen, his father joined the Liverpool Philharmonic. Now living not far from the street where John Lennon was born, Guy became obsessed with The Beatles. And at his new school, there was 'a really cool little group' who inspired him. 'They were a bit like Free. Free meets The Small Faces. They were about sixteen and I remember thinking, I want to be a) in that band, or b) in a band.'

A year later he'd achieved b), at least. His younger brother played the drums, a mate played bass, Guy played guitar. A year after that and he'd joined 'a proper band' – Hambi and the Dance, signed to Virgin. He must have known he was talented, because he was just fifteen and the others were in their early twenties. But it 'wasn't really happening' for Hambi, so in 1981, Guy left and, encouraged by his father, went back to London to do a degree in composition and piano at the Guildhall School of Music. He got on to a jazzier track and at eighteen thought for a while he might be a jazz musician. Then he met a few. 'It put me off. Older guys. I realised that most jazz musicians were extremely sad.' He had a period of post-grad poverty, playing the piano in bars around town, living rent-free with a friend, even signing on for a couple of months. Then came his first big break, playing keyboards for Julian Cope in The Teardrop Explodes, and going on tour for the first time to Japan, where Julian was a big star. 'It was eye opening. Seeing fans and groupies and all that side of it.' At that stage, Guy thought he'd be fronting a band of his own one day, and this fantasy remained alive as he played keyboards first for The Waterboys and then for World Party. And when Guy left the latter and at last formed his own group, The Lemon Trees, which he fronted on guitar, he still thought he had a chance. 'But then, pretty rapidly, I realised I didn't have the necessary credentials to front the band: a) I wasn't a good enough singer and b) I wasn't Mr Charisma on stage. I needed to find a partner who could be the pop star I couldn't be, I suppose.'

For Tim and David, looking for a composer to make songs out of Rob's powerful poetry, finding

Guy was 'a bit of divine intervention'. His tape had been sent over by two separate individuals who they knew and respected, so they felt they had to listen to it. 'We were wading through endless shit,' David remembers. 'And then suddenly the Guy stuff arrived.'

The managers introduced Guy and Rob to each other in a studio in north London. Rob, who had been working with 'drug buddies and other people I was never going to hit it off with' had been shown a piece of paper with lots of names of potential collaborators on it.

'And I just saw "Guy Chambers",' he says, 'and I went, "That's him." No, I hadn't heard his music. I still haven't heard his pre-me music. I intuitively knew he was the person.'

'It just worked instantly,' says David Enthoven. 'After two days they played us the stuff and we thought it was pop heaven, basically. Music heaven. All this repressed energy suddenly went...' David tails off, lost for words at the vision of successful creative fusion. 'Because we'd suddenly got on the railway track. And the train was pulling out of the station at a remarkable pace.'

'Tee yah yee hey hey hey hey yah'

It's a dazzling sunny day in Stockholm, but the only members of the party up to take advantage of the elaborate breakfast buffet are security guards Marv and Jonah. A little later, Franksy pitches up. He's been working out in the gym, 'preserving the old body', he says with a rueful smile. He's 44. His nickname, 'Prince of Darkness', is an ironic moniker for a man with kind, droopy eyes and a smile that curls slowly up to express his appreciation of a good story. He has a catalogue of his own, dating back to his days as a performer in the Bristol of the seventies, playing bass in a punk rhythm and blues band called The Wild Beasts.

It was in Germany with Depeche Mode that Franksy collapsed at a gig and carried on working for five shows without seeing a doctor. When he got to Berlin he went to consult a neurologist, who did a brain scan and told him he'd had a massive brain haemorrhage and he had to go immediately into intensive care. 'I said, "You're having a laugh, aren't you? We're doing a gig at the Olympia tonight." Fortunately they sent the people down in white coats to drag me back. I was that ill that they said potentially getting out of bed was fatal.'

On the legendary later Depeche tour of '93/4, which went twice round the world and was documented as 'the most debauched rock and roll tour ever' by Q magazine, Franksy met his current wife, who was then the group's American travel agent. They had only ever spoken on the phone until she appeared in Mexico. 'I was expecting this middle-aged Laura Ashley frumpy old lady who was just a brilliant laugh – and suddenly this real babe turns up.' But with a professional relationship to maintain, things had to be kept secret. 'She would hide in the wardrobe when people came into my room. Check into the hotel under an assumed name.'

For all his larger-than-life anecdotes, Franksy has a key role in the business of getting Rob on stage. 'David likes to think of the whole regime as a sort of military organisation,' he says. 'I suppose I'm akin to somewhere between captain and lieutenant.' His daily call sheet, slipped under the doors of their rooms every evening, gives his talented charges their marching orders in light-hearted style.

The band surface slowly in their five-star hotel rooms, preserving their energy for their crucial first gig tonight. Rob stays in bed till after lunch, as does Gary. The guitarist admits there is some truth to the band's other running joke about him – that when he's not eating junk food he's asleep: 'Bed is very, very important to me.'

By 3.30 they're all down in the lobby and ready to go. As they follow Franksy out to the minibuses, they pass the usual little cluster of female fans, with one thing on their mind. 'Is Robbie coming?' 'Is Robbie here?' they ask. Franksy ignores them; he's on his mobile to production manager Wob Roberts, putting finishing touches to the stage at the Isstadion. Rob's changed his set again and this is causing problems. 'I don't know what to say, Wob,' counsels the Prince of Darkness gently. 'If he wants to change it, he wants to change it...

'I swear I
thought
I was the
Elephant
Man for a
good
couple of
years.'

Once at the venue, the band vanish to their dressing rooms in the network of lino-floored corridors backstage. Between 'MALE/HOSPITALITY' and 'FEMALE', Rob's private sanctum is all laid out and ready. There are black plastic couches around two low blue tables. A square candle sits on one, a big bowl of fruit on another: grapes, Kiwi fruit, melon, pineapple, strawbs, a pomegranate. There are ashtrays, Orbit gum, Ricola cough lozenges. Behind, two heavily shaded lamps and plants in white tubs. In two full-length wardrobes are all his outfits: suits, shirts, trousers, coats. A black strap-on tie. Lying on the shoes below, two footballs.

Up at the end, to the right of the full-length mirror, is a make-up table on which sits a CD player and a stack of CDs. Shea Seger is the top one. Four packs of Silk Cut. Six bottles of Volvic. A Peanut Butter Crunch Bar, an Apple Cobbler Crunch Bar (with yoghurt coating). Fudge hair putty. Clarins Masque 'Anti-Soif', Fluide Désaltérant, Eclat du Jour Energising Morning Cream and Huile Orchidée Bleue face treatment. Elizabeth Arden Eight Hour Cream. A box of Kleenex.

In the production office along the corridor, there's a contrastingly busy scene. As accountant Tom counts cash and enters figures into his laptop, Wob Roberts talks urgently into his mobile. His black silk shirt (custom made in Singapore) is almost as shiny as his shoulder-length dark hair. In his right ear is a diamond stud. One-time bass guitarist in a seventies prog-rock band, Wob has progressed through the-atrical electrician and guitar tech (for Nik Kershaw) in the eighties, to the moment in the late nineties where Tim and David called him to say, 'We've got this artist called Robbie Williams. We need a produc-tion manager. D'you want to do it?' Now he's responsible for the smooth running of the crew's extraordinary daily operation: not just getting the set up in the morning, but down again after the gig and back into the trucks in time to drive on overnight to the next venue. And tonight, on the very first gig of the tour, Rob's suddenly decided to put a new song in his set; sound, lighting and video programmes have to be completely reorganised and they're only four hours away from putting him on stage in front of 7,000 people.

Outside in the arena, spotlights swivel through the smoky air, washing the empty rows of seats that mount diagonally from floor to ceiling. 'Tee yah yee hey hey hey hey yah,' goes a guy with poppy eyes and a monk's haircut into Robbie's central micro-phone. 'Yah one one one hey yeah,' he continues, moving along to Fil's. Guitarist Gary wanders on stage and embraces another of the T-shirted gang.

When the rest of the band have arrived for the soundcheck they get to grips with Rob's latest change of plan. 'Sorry,' Guy tells the band, 'we're going to have to learn "Live And Let Die", I'm afraid'. Yolanda's not happy, not feeling well anyway – she's got a streaming cold. In the ever-changing purplish-reddish light they rehearse the new song, Katie and Tessa giving it their all with, 'You know you did, you kno-ow you did.'

There's an odd anxiety in the air.

Wounded Animal

Drum tech Mick Winder is about to experience a terrible case of déjà vu. He's not a regular with the crew, and the last time he worked with the Robbie operation was here in Stockholm on an unforgettable night. Now, after soundcheck, as he crouches on stage making the final adjustments to Chris's drum set, Wob appears beside him. There's a problem, he says. Can't say what it is, but Rob has called the entire band and crew into the male dressing room to make an announcement.

As everyone stands around expectantly, discussing what this could possibly be about, Rob comes in. He looks round at them all, slowly. He can't explain why, he tells them, but he just can't do it, he can't go on stage. Not tonight. Sorry. The show will have to be cancelled. There's a collective gasp. He's got to be joking, Mick thinks. This can't be happening again.

Two years ago, at the start of another European tour, in this very same city of Stockholm, Rob refused point-blank to go on stage. Later that evening the whole tour was cancelled and Rob flew back to England. He was at the end of his tether, exhausted and ill, in a state of total collapse.

Rob had flown direct from a particularly gruelling promotional trip round America to start in Europe. The final show had been in Austin, Texas.

'After the gig,' says Gabby Chelmicka, who was Rob's PA at the time and is now a director of IE, 'he went to explore Austin's nightlife and some girls went back to his room. So he ended up staying up all night and he was in a terrible state the next morning.'

'He got completely shit-faced that night,' says David Enthoven, 'which is fair enough. But I remember the next morning seeing his little face in the back of the limo, just not wanting to go to Stockholm. I sort of sensed there was going to be a problem. It was like sending a little boy off to school.'

'So we got to Austin airport,' Gabby continues, 'and he was all over the place. He was lying down at the airport, couldn't do anything. And I had my daughter Ella with me at the time; I was travelling with her. I said to him, "Just push the pushchair through departures," because he could hardly stand. His knuckles were white on the handle. He wanted to go back to the hotel and get on the plane with Tim and David, who were flying back to London. But we managed to get him on the flight, Franksy got everyone an upgrade to first class, and he slept all the way. We got to Stockholm early on Sunday morning and the gig was on Monday night.'

Since the end of his previous UK tour, two crew members whom Rob was particularly fond of had

had to leave the entourage. 'We hadn't had a chance to tell Rob about this,' says Gabby. 'It wasn't that we didn't want to, the opportunity just hadn't arisen. So we got to the gig on Monday afternoon and when Rob realised this pair were no longer there he went ballistic. Screamed and shouted and everything. I think in a way that was the straw that broke the camel's back. He wasn't feeling well; he was terribly jetlagged and he'd been complaining about a sore throat all day. He simply broke down and said, "I'm not going on stage tonight."'

Gabby, Guy and the band all got together to persuade Rob to change his mind. And under pressure, he did. 'He said, "OK, I'll do it. I feel like shit, but I'll do it." At this stage the auditorium was full; everyone was there. Then five minutes later he said, "I can't do it. I feel like shit."' Gabby called another meeting with the band, and they all tried to talk Rob into going on stage.' "We'll carry you, Rob, it'll be all right." He said, "All right, I'll do it." But then he wouldn't again.' So the concert was called off. Band and star left the venue. Production manager Wob was left to tell the audience that Robbie wasn't appearing. A doctor was called to Rob's hotel. Later that evening, the star cancelled the whole tour. 'He was just lying there watching telly, not appearing to care, and he just said, "I'm not going to do any of this tour,"' Gabby remembers. 'All this time there was a hotline between me and Tim in London. "It's OK, he's doing it." "No, he's not." "Yes, he is." It was horrible.'

As far as Rob was concerned it was his decision to make, about his performance. Both band and crew were going to get paid. If he couldn't do it, he couldn't do it. 'Put it this way,' he says, 'I turned up in Sweden and there was no way I could get on stage. No way I could perform. No way I could present myself. What I thought I was at the time and what I thought I looked like. I swear I thought I was the Elephant Man for a good couple of years. My job is to get up on stage and be judged. And the judgements I was passing against myself at that time were terrible.'

Rob flew back to his mother in Stoke-on-Trent. 'I cried all the way home on that flight to Manchester,' Gabby says. 'He hadn't said a word to me. He played backgammon or cards with Chris Sharrock the whole way. He looked like he didn't care but he was actually close to a total breakdown.' David puts it another way. He was 'a wounded animal'. 'He was exhausted. This was a guy who was in the midst of his addictions and drinking, living in an illness and in deep denial. He couldn't possibly admit that it was anything to do with him. But the reason he was exhausted was because he was stuffing things up his nose and drinking too much.'

Having dropped the latest bombshell, Rob walks slowly out of the room. Everyone starts reacting frantically. Production manager Wob is running out screaming instructions. Franksy's going mad on his mobile. The band have all got their coats on and are saying, 'We're going home.'

As Mick wanders aimlessly back towards the now redundant stage, Franksy runs after him and calls him back into the dressing room. Before Rob returns to his hotel, Franksy says, he would like a private word. Mick follows the tour manager in, not sure what's going on. Franksy and Josie stand to one side with serious faces. Rob looks unhappy. He looks up at the drum tech. Is he going to apologise for putting him in this position twice? 'Listen, Mick,' he says, 'I don't want you to think it's anything to do with you or whatever, I just need to tell you ... that you're being wound up.'

Franksy, Josie and David break into howls of laughter.

'You little bastard!' says Mick, as Rob laughs too and hugs his technician. 'I was thinking this stinks a little bit here. But you got me.'

For David the wind-up feels quite serious, because they are all in Stockholm again, the scene of the earlier, darker disaster. The joke is like a purging, he thinks. This time it's different, Rob is healthy. 'It was done with some relief on my part,' says Rob, 'because this time I knew I could go on stage.'

Still laughing, everyone heads down to catering for supper. Besides cooking breakfast and lunch for the crew, chief chef Graham Morrisson and his team prepare everyone a four-course evening meal, on tables with tablecloths and candles and napkins. Tonight's printed menu offers carrot and dill soup or salad nicoise; braised beef, escalope of turkey, sea bream, spinach and goat's cheese filo parcels, spaghetti with courgettes, red peppers and kalamata olives; chocolate cheesecake, fresh fruit salad and cheese board. All served in a requisitioned changing room with coat hangers still visible on the row of hooks along the wall.

Out at the front of the venue, of course, the fans know nothing about all this backstage malarkey, as they queue to buy lager in plastic pint mugs, or hamburgers in limp buns, or a souvenir from the Robbie merchandise stall on the left of the foyer (supervised by Richie Stevenson and Waff Walker, who are part of the crew, but travel separately with their stuff in a van). There are Robbie scarves, Robbie hats, Robbie jackets, Robbie football shirts like the ones on Sing When You're Winning, Robbie fleeces, Robbie knickers and pants, Robbie bowling and plimsoll bags, Robbie mugs, Robbie posters and pendants, Robbie tour programmes, even a Robbie keying-cum-bottle opener (which looks unfortunately, Franksy jokes, considering the star's current situation, like a giant coke spoon).

The arena, meanwhile, is just about full. In front of the huge black curtain – the kabuki – that hides Robbie's set, Swedish support band Mew are playing. When they finish, the lights go up. A screen is lowered. A video shows a blonde gazing longingly at photocopies of Robbie; then he turns up at the door in silhouette and autographs the top photocopy.

'I love getting applause.
I think people by nature
want people to say, "You're
good." Everybody does.

I'm no exception to that.

I feel important when
people clap.

It's just basically making
showing off a fine art.

That's what I've done.
I've made showing off
a fine art.'

Excitement mounts as the public announcements start. The joke about H from Steps doesn't work with this audience, but it doesn't matter, for now the roving spotlights have come on, raking across the crowd, turning the thousand heads on the floor below into tiny round silhouettes. 'Robbie! Robbie!' goes the Carmina Burana tape. 'Robbie! Robbie!' echoes a group of eager Swedes. Then in a dazzling series of white light flashes, the kabuki drops to reveal the completely bare stage. Slowly, from the roof, the band is lowered on the riser. Their descent from the heights is extraordinary, almost dream-like. Fil and Gary and Yolanda run off to their positions – and behind, suddenly, here is Rob, now become Robbie, the performer, projected in his luminous-tendrilled throne, up through the raised floor of the back of the set and into the silver cage in the middle. He gets slowly to his feet and swaggers across to and down the silver steps to the right of the stage. The front half of the crowd on the floor below is already jumping up and down, waving their arms in the air like wild things. It's a critical moment: Rob's first steps on to the stage break the spell of the disastrous past and, as it will transpire, herald a new kind of tour, indeed a new kind of Rob. But the audience knows nothing of this; they are just enjoying the show.

'My name is Robbie Williams,' he says. 'I want to entertain you, and you, you, you…' And he's into his set, strutting his jumping, sauntering, right-leg-jigging, microphone-stand-bending, audience-commanding stuff. Around him, his band members do their individual things. To his left stands Gary, virtually immobile as he plays; to his right Fil races around the stage like a wild thing, leaping up on the big black speakers on the edge of the stage, jumping down, dancing like a turbo-charged pogo stick, strumming with wide-armed extravagance. Behind is Yolanda, leaning back funkily, making occasional little pantherish dashes across the stage. Then the tableau at the back: Claire, left, grinning and bobbing at her keyboard stack; little Chris, barely visible behind his drums (the sticks fly up occasionally, to be expertly caught); curly-haired Guy nodding benignly from his keyboards on the right, 'like the schoolteacher looking down on everyone,' says Franksy. Away over to the far right, backing singers Katie and Tess croon into their upright mikes.

'One hand in the air, two hands in the air,' Robbie orders his crowd. And right around the oval they obey him, this supremely charismatic manikin, so far away.

It's hard to believe that he's still hating it, but really he is. 'I'd had complete self-loathing for quite some time,' he says later, 'and along with that comes no confidence. When you've got no confidence and you've got to get up on stage every night it becomes a task, a real hard task. The only thing that honestly motivated me at the time to get up there – and I don't want to sound like a money-grabber – was money. Because I thought I'd got to make as much as possible before everybody realised I was shit and they turned their backs on me. Because I thought that was inevitable.'

'Thank God Britney Spears was there,' says David, 'because he gave a great performance – really for her. She stood by the side of the stage, and he was really going for it. I knew he wasn't enjoying it – he'll give me a kind of grimace on the edge of the stage – yet it was a really slick performance.'

The Swedes are enthusiastic, but by no means eating out of his hand. Robbie does 'Old Before I Die' and 'Lazy Days', but the next thing to get them really going is 'Hey Jude'. When 'Better Man' follows the tempo slows, and all around the arena people wave lighters, tiny swaying flames in the darkness. Then a quiet little bow and, 'Tak,' the Swedish for 'thank you'.

That one gesture, saying thank you in Swedish, finally gets the cheer Rob needs. 'You feeling all right?' he asks, and there's an amazing scream, right below him. 'Did you just come?' he laughs. 'Can somebody come with a bucket and a shovel – it's all wet down there.'

Their returning laughter fills the stadium. Now, he says, he's going to sing them a song they know. They roar approval. 'You liars!' he berates them cheerfully. 'You've never heard it.' The people at the front have his first two albums, the people at the back have only got his third album, so they don't know it. 'No, no,' he adds, sensing immediately that this jokey insult hasn't gone down that well, that he's in danger of losing all the ground he's just made up, that he needs to smile at them and be gracious and win them back with his magical charm.

'People at the back, I've got nothing but love for you. Welcome to the Robbie Williams show.'

Rob bows to the cheers at the end of 'Kids', then he's off, right behind his band, down the steps lit by Franksy's torch to gulp mineral water from the bottle and be towelled dry by the French wardrobe girl with the Louise Brooks bob of black hair. 'More! More! More!' chant the crowd from the front of stage. Brow mopped, Rob's out of his suit, into a white T-shirt, and back out there.

'Ladies and gentlemen,' he tells them, 'it's some-body's birthday tomorrow.' He grins his little-boy grin as they cheer. Nods, chews, shrugs urbanely. 'Thank you very much,' he tells them. Then: 'Stop, stop!' He's looking up towards the side of the arena. 'I've just seen someone with their coat on, leaving. Ladies and gentlemen, this birthday boy is not very happy. We'll give them a big "Fuck off". One, two, three – fuck off!' Then, after a perfectly timed beat, 'And now a ballad.'

'You're really great tonight,' he fibs at the end of 'She's The One'. 'I feel as if I've left a bit of my heart with you. Ladies and gentlemen, I want to see your hands in the air.'

And this time the forest of fingers for 'Millennium' stretches out to become a sea. Here and there above the surface float swaying enraptured young mermaids. From the other side of the stage David's huge grin is visible. The Stockholm jinx has been overcome. He and Josie clap their hands wildly over their heads.

After the gig, as Rob and the band slump down in their dressing rooms backstage, with tea or beer or champagne à choix, the crew strip to the waist and get to work unravelling all their hard work of earlier, putting instruments and monitors back in cases, lowering lighting trusses and cycloramas to the stage, dismantling and packing everything away in the RW 'flight cases', to be pushed up the long ramp to the waiting trucks outside.

As this labour of love continues, on into the small hours, Rob and the band sweep back to the hotel, then on to the post-gig bash at Stockholm's Café Opera, 400 yards along the river frontage from the Grand.

Rob is the star guest, eagerly expected by the chattering crowd of night people sitting round tables in the elegant, plant-filled, glass-walled salon. The band are obviously invited too, as are Franksy and Tom. As the accountant makes his way across the frozen cobbles towards the brightly lit scene he's accosted by two willowy young blondes who look as if they've wandered out of Elvira Madigan. It's not something that would happen to him in the normal run of things. But they have a question he's well used to on tour. Is Robb-ieeee coming to the party?

Tom is happy to stop and chat to them for a moment. 'If you hang around, you might see him.'
As he walks on, Tom laughs. 'Fans, dude,' he says. But he's hoping the three 'Bird Alert' chicks from last night will turn up at the party. It was he, it transpires, who was responsible for them being in the hotel. He's been e-mailing them since the last time he was in Stockholm on a tour.

The hosts of the party, the Swedish branch of Robbie's record company EMI, are waiting at the end of the restaurant, up at a VIP table behind a rope on a dais. If Rob is coming, he's in for a shock. In the middle of the table is a row of glinting vodka bottles, surrounded by a subsidiary stash of tonic. A waitress goes round with champagne. And who comes here, tripping from the disco room up the steps to the right? The 'Bird Alert' trio! Tom goes over with arms outstretched to greet them.

After twenty minutes or so, Rob walks in, with Josie, David and his security guys in tow, looking like a cross between a dignitary and an invalid in his coat and woolly hat. His eyes dart powerfully over the scene, from one tour member to another, taking in their relaxed faces and glasses of booze... There's a momentary frisson of uncertainty from the band and entourage about the new rules of the game. Does this count as a confined space? Will Rob mind, be

tempted, upset? Franksy's seen Rob make the decision to give up drink and drugs before. 'Then he'd
get back to the bar, everyone else was there drinking
and there was a party going, and suddenly he decides
he's going to have a beer. And once he's had a couple
of beers, without knowing too much about how it
works mentally for him, once you start, the trigger
has gone and then you move on to other things.'

One or two push their drinks gingerly away. But
Rob is OK. They're having a good time, why
shouldn't they? It's not difficult for him to see them
drinking tonight. He heads round the table to catch
up with his Swedish team and stays just long enough
for everyone to sing 'Happy Birthday'.

Also present are the five members of the documentary team who are going to be following Rob
on his tour. Assistant director Katie Bailiff is already
deeply intrigued by the whole Rob conundrum. She
herself is from Morecambe and thinks Rob is very
like the lads she grew up with at home. She finds
herself talking to him like that. He's a superstar, yet
he's also, in some ways, just a 26-year-old lad. 'He's a
combination of two or three of my friends when I
was sixteen. I've got one who's very charming and
flirty, and that's what he's like. He makes eye contact
with you when you look at him and makes you
feel… He kisses you on the cheek and he'll give you
a hug.' But she thinks he should really have somebody on the tour with him he's not paying, who is
just a mate.

Guy's a bit disappointed that that cute girl over there was so off with Rob. 'He told her it was his birthday, and asked whether she was at the gig. She just said "yes", nothing else. Didn't even offer him a birthday kiss.'

Fil, meanwhile, is engaged in more purposeful conversation, sparkling with his skinny, snake-eyed charm as he chats up the prettiest of the Bird Alert trio. Before the evening is out, this has progressed to heavy public snogging. Tom, meanwhile, despite heroic efforts on the dance floor, is not getting very far with her less glamorous mates.

At 2.30 a.m., the two willowy blondes are still outside the hotel, shivering together on a recessed ledge just along from the main revolving doors to the lobby. What on earth are they doing, still out in this bitter cold?

'I know,' admits Katarina with a laugh. 'It's pretty silly. I've seen all the girls standing outside Backstreet Boys and I think, Oh my God, what are they doing? I would never do that. But Robbie is… is …'

'Special.'

'He's very special. He has been my idol since I was very little. Maybe ten or something.'

What time is he leaving tomorrow? they want to know.

And sure enough, they're there the next day, Katarina faithfully waiting for her idol at the centre of the little crowd outside the revolving doors at lunchtime. As he strides out to his car, Robbie stops to sign a couple of autographs – but sadly, not theirs.

He's lived with the adoration of thousands of young females since he was sixteen and is quite used to it by now. Despite their adamance that he is different and they are a different kind of fan, he refuses to see himself (or them) as special. 'It's not just me. They'd be there for Steps or Westlife if they were in town. They wait for everybody,' he insists wearily.

3

'I've never known
that I haven't wanted
to perform or wanted
to sing or act.

I can't remember a
time that it came
across me. It's just in
my bones. It's always
been in my bones.'

ORANGE JUICE RAVE

While Wob, the crew, and the five trucks full of equipment go ahead overnight by road, Rob and the band make the short flight (staffed by reassuringly ancient air hostesses) out above the massed tiny islands of the Stockholm archipelago and down over a most dazzling silver-gold sea – the huge new Denmark–Sweden bridge firmly in view – to land with a bump in Copenhagen.

Yolanda's nose is firmly in a fat paperback – *Memoirs of a Geisha*. 'I'm an avid reader,' she says, almost apologetically, flashing her huge smile. It's one of her favourite things about touring, that she gets the time to read. Back home in Tottenham Hale, with two kids and a husband to look after, she doesn't really – she winces – get much of a chance.

Fil, meanwhile, is sleeping. He took the prettiest Bird Alert back to his hotel room last night, Tom says, his envy ill concealed in his laughter.

It's Rob's birthday today and a day off from gigs, so tonight there's going to be some kind of celebration in Rob's honour. As the coach hired for the band leaves the airport and slides on to the motorway into Copenhagen, there's speculation among the band members about what kind of thing it might be. 'An orange juice rave?'

As the coach slows down in the cycle-heavy traffic of the central city, Franksy gets up on the microphone at the front of the bus to explain. Rob's party is going to be in a club a few minutes from the hotel, with 'a surprise band' playing. 'And hopefully Rob will turn up and do something as well…'

'At his own party!' laughs Claire from the other end of the bus.

'Otherwise,' the Prince of Darkness continues, 'I hope you all have a nice time in Copenhagen. Don't forget Christiania is here.' There are knowing chuckles from the band at the mention of the city's famous hippy island, where blocks of hash are sold openly on 'Pusher Street'. 'Be very, very careful,' Franksy warns, 'if you go there. Don't be too conspicuous, or hang around in packs, or say you're English and playing in a band. Apart from that, have a lovely evening in Copenhagen.'

But by the time the band members gather downstairs in the hotel bar at nine, the party is in disarray. Rob's been told that the paparazzi have found out and are going to be besieging the place, so he's not going. Guy's wife has turned up from London, so he's not going. Drummer Chris isn't going either. Maybe, laughs Fil, he went to Christiania and didn't come back. But anyway, the 'surprise band' now won't be appearing. So does everyone still want to go? asks Franksy. Perhaps we should all just go up to Rob's room? suggests Gary. We can't all go up, says

Fil, and anyway, he'll be drinking water. So yes, the majority do want to go and at least have a look at the party. As the group head out of the front door, Katie Kissoon backs discreetly into the lift.

At the club, the crew have turned out in force, many, alarmingly, in brightly coloured clothes. They mix enthusiastically with the specially invited local crowd, though which are celebs and which are mere mortals it's hard to tell. Certainly, there are some fab haircuts. Everyone's desperate for a band, and in the end one is raked together by inebriated members of the crew; Fil is its only serious member.

'Ladies and gentlemen,' announces lead singer 'Little Jez' (the large-headed, short Yorkshireman who is Gary's guitar tech). 'Nirvhana!'

A noise like a street full of banging dustbin lids ensues. 'Batley Entertainments live!' yells Jez over the racket. Fil's face has been twisting into more and more of a grimace at the din his fellow band members are making. 'No, no, no-o-o!' he groans, as he gets to his feet and leaves the stage.

And Rob never makes it. He stays back in his room, playing cards with Marv, Jonah, David, Josie, Guy, Chris, plus, tonight, Guy's wife Emma. 'It was surreal,' says Guy. 'This group of us sitting around in Rob's room playing Uno and drinking water. And people at home would probably think he was spending his birthday off his face in some club shagging two birds.' Guy chuckles. 'Which he might well have been another year.'

'Birthdays don't hold any significance for me anyway,' says Rob. 'It just so happens to be the day I was born on and that's it. So there was no big, "And tonight he's not drinking, perhaps he should be, perhaps he misses it because it's his birthday." It was just another tour night.

'I have been completely and utterly bonkers on my birthday, yeah. It's an added excuse or free ticket to go mad for a couple of days. But I could have that free ticket just because it was Tuesday, or a full moon. Particularly a full moon. That was always the best excuse. "Wow, it's a full moon. That makes me mad because I'm in line with all that spiritual stuff, so I'll buy an extra three grams tonight." '

Self-esteem

It's Wednesday 14 February. Valentine's Day in Copenhagen. The streets are full of made-up bunches of flowers. Inflatable red heart-shaped balloons reading Jeg Elsker Dig fly in bunches from the corners of market stalls. The venue is a smaller, flatter stadium than Stockholm. Red roses stand in tall vases in the corporate hospitality area to one side.

In his dressing room before the show, Rob seems in a relaxed mood, slumped back on one of the leatherette couches, strumming away at his guitar and talking about his progression from undervalued member of Take That to his current superstardom.

'When Tim and David first came to my flat I was just this coke and beer monster,' he remembers with a laugh. 'Unwashed with a beard coming through and big hair, just embarrassing really. I sat down with them and started reciting this poetry that I'd written. And I could see their faces. I knew that this poetry worked, because many times, off my face, I used to recite it in people's bathrooms, or, you know, at parties. I can always remember me being off my face and grabbing Bono and George Michael and making them go to a separate room to hear my lyrics. And it worked with Tim and David too. I could see their faces light up.

'I started writing it when I was in Take That. I knew I had some talent, because I used to do melody lines. I used to write these songs in my head. I remember going down Dean Street in Manchester, where there's just lots of prostitutes. And I wrote about them. And I sang this song down the phone to Gary Barlow, going, "What do you think?" There was just a silence at the other end.' Rob slips into mimicking Barlow's voice. 'Then "It's all right, that, lad." Then he said to somebody else, "That Robbie's started writing stuff. It would be all right if we were in a rock and roll band."

'Then I wrote a rap on the end of a song called "Once You've Tasted Love", which was a Take That non-hit in the early days. I can always remember hearing it on the radio and crying, because something that I'd done was on the radio. I was in the back of a van going down the M6 at the time. But it became very apparent that anything that you tried to do writing-wise wouldn't be encouraged. I learnt from then on that that was not my role. Plus I didn't think I was very good at it, so I didn't bother.

'Then, I can remember we were in Dusseldorf, in the middle of a European tour with Take That, and I was really sad. About everything that was going on around me, the position I'd put myself in. So I started writing poetry to release some of it. I just thought, I am worthwhile, I have a talent.'

This self-doubting private man is a very different creature to the one that was whipping up the crowds so expertly two nights ago in Stockholm. But rather than leave the subject of his insecurity, or consign it firmly to the past, he looks up with eyes that are no longer restless and avoiding, but meet yours with transparent sincerity.

'You know,' he says, 'I don't hold anything I've done with any esteem whatsoever – it's a disease I've got. I find it very difficult to have any self-worth about anything that I've created. Even more so when I'm standing up in front of all those people. It's such a damn shame. It's such a real big shame that my self-worth is such that I can't sit back and actually enjoy what's going on. I'm in a big arena, they're singing my songs back to me. For somebody that enjoys this it would be amazing.

'I developed a front a long time ago that hid my insecurities and that front is one hundred times bigger than myself. Whatever picture I paint of who they think I am, which is somebody I put up a shield to protect myself from – cocky, cheeky, confident, arrogant – is not who I am. Rob is different from Robbie. Robbie is the one who gets on stage every night and goes, "Let me entertain you." If I'm off-stage I wouldn't ask anybody if I could entertain them.' He grins endearingly. 'I'd be scared if they said "no".'

Maintaining this performance has taken its toll, though – Rob is heartily tired of touring.

'How many times do I have to do this,' he muses, 'before I actually finally realise that it makes me ill? Other people seem to manage very well. But I look at Madonna and think, Why is she still doing that? What is the constant need to change? She is in her 40s now. She looks great … amazing. But I'm thinking, Why does she still feel the need to do that?'

'I very easily could sabotage everything. I could say, "I hate all of this and I never want to do it again." Then I'd have a year off and say, "Actually, I feel much better now. There's a few things personally in my life that I've sorted out," and perhaps I would enjoy it. But my feeling right now is just to sabotage everything.' He looks over and it's alarmingly clear that he means what he says.

'If it gets too much on this tour, I'll just walk away.'

Praying to Elvis
But when it comes to show time, you couldn't begin to guess at the angst of an hour earlier. The doubting,

unhappy Rob has been replaced by the upbeat Robbie, confidently leading the band, as they prepare for the gig with their backstage warm-up 'huddle' in the corridor outside the dressing rooms. This includes Robbie, the whole band, David, Josie, Flo the French wardrobe mistress, Marv and Jonah the security guys, and anyone else who happens to be around: arms round shoulders in a big circle, knees slightly bent, joining in a performer's prayer to the King of Rock and Roll. No-one, at Rob's particular insistence, is allowed to be outside.

'Elvis,' he leads, 'grant me the serenity to accept the things I cannot change…'

'Aha!' the gang respond, while jerking their knees to the left.

'The courage to change the things I can…'

'Aha!' comes the refrain, as communal knees jerk to the right.

'And the wisdom to know the difference.'

'Thank you very much!' shout the group.

Then, following Franksy and his torch, they troop excitedly off along the line of white arrows taped to the arena floor. Ahead are the cheers and screams of the crowd, all but drowning out the nightly warm-up music: Queen's 'Fat Bottomed Girls'. In this swirling, exciting din the band take their positions on the riser. Rob, meanwhile, waits under the stage in his luminous throne, ready to be launched up into the silver cage at the centre-back of the set.

'Did I say my perfect
dad would be a mixture
of those four? Frank,
Dean, Sammy and
Mohammed Ali?

God, I take that back.

I don't think you can
have a perfect dad.
You can't. Human
beings by their nature
make mistakes. You
just try to be the
best you can be.'

It's a strange, dark little cavernous area, this under-stage room. On the wall facing the stage are framed photos of Rob's heroes, numbered from 1) to 4). They are Frank Sinatra, Sammy Davis Jnr, Mohammed Ali and Dean Martin. As the cheers build to a climax outside, he jogs down past them in his black suit and pays them a ritual homage. 'I kiss them all,' he says, 'because at some point in my life they've given me the courage and the inspiration to make more of myself. You take away the fact that Mohammed Ali was a great athlete, probably the greatest the world's ever known, and what you've got is a man that's so courageous and stood up for his beliefs throughout it all. He was and is a prophet. He was charming and articulate, he was handsome and he was fast. That gives me courage to see somebody like that. And I try and soak up as much of that before I go on stage, because I need it, I really need it.

'Then I kiss Frank Sinatra. He had an amazing voice. I'm also scared of him because he had Mafiosi links and there was a dark side to him that I can pick up on and I can see. But he was also a born leader and people respected him. He was such an amazing performer that he didn't have to do anything. He just sat there and sang. I try and pick up a sense of his character and a sense of his power. Then Dean Martin: I just love him because he was funny. He is the sort of person you'd have wanted as a dad if he wasn't an alcoholic. If you could pick a dad, he'd have the best qualities of all four.'

Rob punches the air, looking up, down, around. Marv and Jonah are right by him. He shakes Marv's hand, then settles himself in his throne, looks straight ahead of him, eyes half-closed, head jogging slightly, arms hanging loosely. 'You're just about to go on stage,' he says, 'and "Fat Bottomed Girls" is playing and the guitar's getting into your soul and the vocals are really pumping.' There's another enormous cheer – the black kabuki curtain must have fallen. He smiles to himself and nods as he hears the throbbing opening chords of 'Let Me Entertain You'. Now Franksy is before him, half-kneeling as if Rob's the Pope. Franksy kisses Rob's hand and Rob kisses Franksy's. Rob smiles to himself as he hears the cheers. His eyes are closed. The radio-mike clenched lightly in his right hand – then, whoa! The counter-weight system has kicked in, and he's off, up there – Robbie Williams the performer – into the bright light of the stage, the view out over 10,000 faces, the waving arms, the sea of excited approval.

He comes out of his cage and strides confidently down the steps.

> Hell is gone and heaven's here
> There's nothing left for you to fear
> Shake your arse come over here
> Now scream...

'Fuck me,' he says at the end of 'Let Me Entertain You', retreating towards the drum dais for a restorative swig of water. By 'Live And Let Die' they're throwing paper cups. 'Better Man' brings a rose to his feet.

As Robbie goes through his routine, picking out individuals to gaze adoringly at, making cheeky faces, telling them they're amazing, asking them to sing 'Happy Birthday' for him, holding out his mike while they sing back his lyrics, laughing as he asks the girls to get their tits out for 'Forever Texas', it seems impossible to believe that it's all a front, that he – at whatever level, Robbie or Rob – is not enjoying it.

Between 'She's The One' and 'Millennium' he stands stock-still and calls, 'Eh-oh!'

'Eeeeeeeh-oh,' they echo faithfully.

'Eeeeeeeeeeeeeeeeeeeeeeeeeeeeeeeeeeeeeeeeeeeeeeeeeh-oh!' He holds the note for ten long seconds. And they reply in kind. The lights come up on their faces as they sing back, this ecstatic bright-eyed army. There's a monumental wail, right below him. 'Mum, you're embarrassing me,' he jokes. 'Millennium' begins, and the familiar sea of fingers fills the arena.

Franksy nods and smiles as he looks out over this astonishing scene. 'Rockin' crowd, innit?' He shakes his head. 'Even a jaded old bloke like me still gets the bloody hairs standing up,' he says, gesturing at the back of his neck.

'I don't know what to say,' Robbie tells them. 'I'm having a great time. I just went to Sweden,' he continues, raising a huge boo as he names that historic enemy, 'and I'm not going to go back up there. I played at this funeral once and this funeral had more life than they did last night. They didn't even know the words to this next song. That's sacrilegious.'

But the Danes know the words. They sing 'Angels' for him tonight, a great roar from the arena as he stands coolly smoking, cupping his hands to his ears in encouragement. At the end of the song his right hand thrusts heavenwards in a fist.

For three seconds he's a statue.

Then he kneels between the speakers. Then he's up and off, the band around him, heading over towards Franksy and his torch. As he strides off backstage, he's looking straight in my direction, raising his eyebrows.

'I enjoyed that,' he mouths.

Unwinding

Back at the hotel there's a post-gig supper – sandwiches and tomato soup – in a panelled dining room beyond the lobby. Through a door in a private room Rob sits quietly with David and Josie. I go in and give him the birthday present I had wrapped yesterday in the lobby of the Stockholm Grand, a pair of red and gold stress balls in a box. Rob immediately starts to play with them, moving them around expertly in his palm, as they jingle-jangle inside.

Next door, the performers are still hyped up yet worn out at the same time. Claire sits with Tess and Katie, who's broken her rule and has a whole glass of wine in front of her. After three sips she reveals, laughing, that she sang the famous hit 'D.I.S.C.O.' – at a session, with her brother.

At the next table Tom is entertaining a model he and Fil met last night at Rob's non-birthday party and a clean-cut young man with black glasses. 'She was a bit thick and really sweet,' says Tom later. 'I was chatting with her at the club and I invited her to the show, with the hopes of me getting something out of it maybe. She showed up and I figured a tall leggy blonde like that would have brought some really pretty girlfriend or her boyfriend – it was Valentine's Day. But sure enough she'd come with her little brother.

'You're not always aware, but Andy Franks makes you aware, when you bring someone foreign into the organisation, you should really let Rob know who they are, out of courtesy. At this point I knew I wasn't going to get anywhere with this girl anyway. So I went into the second room, where Rob and management were sitting, and I said, "Rob, I just wanted to tell you I've got this girl here and her brother – she's really cute." Then I said, straight up, "I don't have a chance with her. She's really hot, but she doesn't seem to be very clued in and I don't seem to be getting anywhere. Please take her off my hands." So he came in after about two minutes. He's walking around kind of eyeing her up from a distance, really trying to give her the eye. But she was so thick she wasn't getting it. Or maybe she just didn't care, I don't know.

'I just went to
Sweden and I'm
not going to go
back up there.

I played at a funeral
once and this
funeral had more
life than they
did in Sweden
last night.'

'She wanted a napkin autograph. So he took her napkin and talked to her a little bit. He autographed it. She walked away. Then he said, "Oh wait, I forgot to put a P.S. note on there." And I was sitting behind her, so when she opened it up I saw the P.S. note in there. It said, "P.S. My name in the hotel is Mr So-and-so and I'm in Room this and I really want to see you tonight." I'm thinking, Yeah, maybe it's finally going to work out. But then she said her brother was feeling a little bit ill and she was going home, so that was that. I guess she was just a nice sweet girl. She did ask me about it, though. She asked what it meant. I'm like, "Come on, you know what it means." She was like, "What does it mean? You mean he wants sex?" I said, "Of course – he's a young man." '

While Rob settles down for a chaste game of Uno in his room, across town, in Copenhagen's smartest nightclub, the local branch of EMI are hosting a party in Robbie's honour. In the absence of the star, the funkily hairstyled night creatures thronging this hip space are eyeing Tom and Fil. The latter is focusing keenly on one of two blondes he picked up on the way in. They are laughing and nodding at each other with all the excitement of brand new friends. By the third bottle of free champagne they are holding hands. And when everyone moves on, at three, clutching red Valentine's heart balloons, to a late night bar up in trendy Nørrebro, they don't stay long. 'The fan and the pop star,' says her friend, shrugging. 'It's inevitable.'

In his new clean life Rob does still have moments of nostalgia. 'There are a few people I miss going out on the piss with and Fil would be one. He's definitely the most hardcore out of the band on the pisshead front. We would always end up in a pickle, but it would always end up being a funny pickle. I don't want to reminisce on my drinking days like they were fun because a lot of them weren't. Ninety-five per cent of them weren't. But he is your best man to get drunk with. He's funny. Very sweet. Amazingly talented. Chicks dig him. Sex is an obsession for him, a compulsion. As it is – was – for me.'

4

'Me on stage and off stage
are chalk and cheese. I'm
a full-of-charisma pop star
on stage. Off stage I've got
bugger all to say to anybody.

I don't know how to speak
to people. And that's been
the case for as long as I can
remember, apart from when
I was growing up. When I
was Robbie-lots-of-mates.'

ROBBIE WORLD

Outside the Copenhagen hotel, Rob's proper rock 'n' roll tour bus is waiting. Behind its darkened windows it has two floors, each with a lounge area. On the lower level, an oblong of padded seats, covered in a multicoloured fabric that was surely dreamed up by someone on a particularly vivid acid trip, surrounds a central table. There's a big TV, loads of videos and DVDs, a kettle, cups, a bowl of fruit, another of sweets, a cupboard full of tea and coffee and sugar and things, and by the door a small toilet. Up the narrow winding stairs, there's a similar lounging area at one end, then rows of curtained-off bunks, two layers on each side, running along to the front, where there's another table between two padded pews above the driver.

As Rob, in his woolly hat, strides through the usual gauntlet of fans with autograph books, he invites a Bjork-lookalike up to the top deck for a minute. 'Because she said something nice to him,' says Josie, 'and Rob wanted to give her his hat.'

Marv and Jonah are keeping a tight hold on the security situation. 'Girl's still on board,' says Marv to Jonah, who stands by the bus's little central door, keeping the other fans at bay. 'She quoted some lyrics from a really obscure song of mine that I like,' says Rob once she's gone. '"Killing Me" off the first album. And I could see in her eyes that she related to it – and how I felt when I'd written that song, or how I felt when I first would play that song back to myself and realise what sort of mess I was in. That touched me. That I'd touched her, because of my words. That means the world to me.'

David, meanwhile, is laughing about Fil, kissing extravagant goodbyes to the blonde from last night as he gets on the band bus behind. 'It's always very heartfelt, the farewell,' he chuckles.

As we race across the flat green countryside, Rob stays upstairs with David, Josie, Guy and drummer Chris, the butcher's boy from Birkenhead. Rob calls him his little mate, 'Even though he's ten years older than me. He stays at my house in London whenever we're rehearsing, whenever we're doing anything really. I enjoy him being about. He's regarded as the best drummer in the world, which is a standard joke around the band. But I've asked a few drummers who they think is the best drummer in the world and it's Chris. He's Keith Moon incarnate.'

Chris disagrees. 'There's no good drummers left,' he says. 'Keith Moon, Buddy Rich, Gene Krupa – they're all dead.' He's been playing drums since he was eight and was given a go on a drum kit on a holiday cruise. The ship's drummer was impressed enough to give the lad an old kit, and within a year Chris was playing in a kids' band. 'It was a great way to get my mum and dad out of the house,' he says. 'They'd never been out till I started playing drums. They used to go to clubs and get a buzz off people saying, "Ooh, look at the little drummer." Because I was nine, but I looked about five.'

Chris has been with Rob since the beginning of Rob's solo career. He'd been in World Party with Guy, and Guy got him in to help with Rob's first demo. 'We did a bit of jamming around and really buzzed off each other,' he remembers. 'Quite inspiring. It's something you can't explain with Rob. The X-factor. Special charisma. It does rub off, because it's like a showy-off thing with me. A cleaner might walk into rehearsals and I'd probably do the same thing. But with Rob it's like that times ten, because he does give it off. That's a true star, someone who can do that.'

In the downstairs lounge, Marv and Jonah sit opposite each other on the psychedelic couches, maintaining their 24-hour guard of the man they refer to as 'the Principal'. Rob has to admit it's a really peculiar way to live. 'Bonkers, actually. But I got them because I used to be that paranoid that I couldn't sleep. I'd have to phone David up in the middle of the night and he'd come over and pick me up. I used to end up going to his house or to a hotel. Then I thought, sod it, I can afford to have somebody around. And hopefully that will dissipate that feeling in the middle of the night just shitting myself with paranoia. George Harrison, Jill Dando, Brad

Pitt. The list is endless of the amount of nutters there are out there. And everybody knows where I live. It's so public. People buzz my door all night, which obviously wakes me up.'

Marv and Jonah are keen to stress they're not the usual kind of bodyguards employed in the music business. They're not overt 'hard men' or 'big bodies', but CP, Close Protection. Other clients of the company of which Jonah and Marv are directors include 'diplomats, top businessmen, politicians'. The nature of how they do their job, they explain, means they work to prevent incidents occurring, rather than curing them once they've taken place. What most security fail to do is the background work, the planning. 'You know,' explains Jonah, 'where the exits to the hotel are: you've worked out routes, timings, seen who's already on the street, fans, press, how many cameras are there.'

About both their client and themselves they are discretion personified. Yes, they say, they did meet in the Marines. And yes, there are units within the Marines that are the equivalent of the SAS.

'Would they be the kind of units that you were involved in?'

'No comment,' says Jonah, with a tight smile. A little later Marv talks about 'a lot of friends in the military who sadly aren't with me any more.'

'When you say not with you any more…?'

'As in they're with the Maker.'

Right.

'And I said, "Listen, look after yourself, but please, go and get a life." And I don't mean "Go and get a life" with an exclamation mark, I genuinely mean that with love.

Go and get a life, because this is no life.'

But they like working for Rob, they say. His set-up is very professional and very family-orientated. 'We've come from the outside,' says Jonah, 'and have been welcomed as part of the family. And there's not a lot of staying up till six o'clock in the morning, parties till God knows what time, wrecking of the rooms, that sort of thing. It just does not happen. Instead we're playing Uno till three, four o'clock in the morning.'

At one point along the road, Rob comes down to use the little toilet. He emerges, half-singing to himself. 'The past is all behind you-ou,' he croons. 'Just wrote a new song,' he tells Guy, who's at the microwave warming up some pasta. 'The past is all behind you-ou... Where's the guitar?'

'Upstairs.'

They go back upstairs and the strains of a creative jam drift down. After a while Rob comes down and pokes his head round the kitchen area. 'There's going to be a game of Uno in half an hour,' he says. 'Ten quid to be in.'

But the coach is at the ferry across to Germany before the call comes, sliding into its allotted space in the fume-filled subterranean lorry section. 'Jonah,' shouts Marv suddenly from upstairs, 'he's going for a walk.'

The pair spring into action. They're hurriedly strapping themselves into their gear: headsets, earphones, baseball caps, a fat pouch at the waist that contains God alone knows what. Then Jonah's outside, demonstrating the techniques of Close Protection in action: checking the other vehicles, the personnel in the cabs of the other vehicles, the entrance to the lift up to the deck. But then comes another shout from Marv. Rob has changed his mind. He's not going for a walk after all. Mission aborted.

Three decks up it's a gloriously bright spring day. David, Franksy and Fil are on the foredeck enjoying the freedom and anonymity Rob cannot. They look much more rock 'n' roll today, Franksy in black baseball cap and leather coat, Fil in wraparound shades and denims. David starts to get into the lift with a quartet of doddery old ladies. 'Taking them back to your room?' calls Franksy and David backs out. There's lots of laughter at the thought of these wind-jacketed, stooping 70-somethings being David's groupies.

As the two tour buses leave the ferry, all five of the documentary film crew pile on to Rob's bus, plus cameras and huge fluffy sound dogs – a weighty posse of flies on the wall. A few miles down the road and Rob reappears on the stairs. 'Have you got any money?' he asks. It's ten quid to be in on the game of Uno that starts in five minutes.

Everyone sits around the table in the little cabin upstairs. Though he's casually dressed in T-shirt and jeans, Rob seems strangely unrelaxed today, gyrating the two jangling stress balls round and round in his palms, his glance fluttering around the tiny lounge as if following a trapped butterfly. He chain smokes, and the unease is tangible. But you can't help warming to him. He's doing his level best, short of having a drink, to make things easy between all these people he's got around him, that his celebrity has forced on him. 'Uno!' Rob shouts. He's won. Then: 'Uno!' He's won again.

When you get 250 points you're out of the game. But the bus has arrived in Hamburg before anybody has anywhere near reached this total. 'Right, what we're going to do,' Rob tells the group, 'is meet in my room in five minutes and finish the game – OK.' He smiles his famous curling smile and makes the sort of powerful gesture he makes on stage at the end of 'No Regrets', like a film director's cut, each hand moving out and down, forefingers outstretched. 'Because it's my tour.'

So at 6.30 on the dot, everyone meets in Rob's suite in this latest splendid hotel, whose huge down-stairs lobby, with its gilt-framed pictures of mythical landscapes, pink and blue fleur-de-lis carpet and sedate groups of deep red armchairs, is already crowded with dolled-up groups of German fans. Rob is smoking again, working with the stress balls. 'Glass table,' he observes to Josie with a wry smile, as the first round of cards are dealt out.

The Uno game continues. Having reconvened us, Rob isn't going to send us away, but the intimacy of the bus has gone, and Rob seems to be just politely doing his duty now. At one point he gets up, goes to the tall window and opens it. Freezing air floods in. The room becomes cold, and the mournful edginess of the occasion is made worse. Nobody says, as they would in any other situation, 'Hey, Rob, let's shut the bloody window, shall we?'

A steak arrives on a trolley with a flower in a vase. Rob stands up, brings it back to the card table and scoffs it hurriedly as we play. You can sense his desire for release from all this, all these people around him, endlessly wanting a bit of him.

'People don't say no to him,' says Josie, 'because he doesn't ask for ludicrous things. He doesn't have outrageous demands. He works hard and there's not much to say no to him for.'

'I always say to Rob,' says David, '"If you wanted an elephant to keep you amused backstage, I'd go and find an elephant." Making a joke of it, but it's true. It's all about keeping him happy, really. And it sounds very pandering, but actually it's not, because we all know at the end of the day, come nine o'clock at night, he's got to get up there and do his stuff. And that's a pretty damn stressful job. So frankly if he wants to go and play crazy golf, if he wants to go and go-kart, play football, whatever he wants to do, we'll do it. He calls it Robbie World, not Robert World, where he's basically got all these people who will sort every whim he wants out. And that's OK, but it's not really real. You can't live like that. A lot of times a lot of bands fall into the fact that they live in this extraordinary world. But you're out doing a job for a specific period of time, and the boss gets looked after, because the boss delivers the bacon.'

'He obviously can't just walk the streets and go shopping like everyone else,' says Gabby Chelmicka. 'Andy Franks is brilliant at sorting out distractions; we call him Mr Extra Curricular.'

So tonight, Franksy's organised a group trip to see the recently released Hannibal at Hamburg's English cinema – but it's not the casual event ordinary folk experience. Jonah and Marv have already excused themselves from the Uno game to go and reconnoitre the space, check the exits and entrances, see who's in the foyer and on the street outside. And by the time Rob and the band turn up, Operation Cinema Visit is thoroughly in place. The tour bus stops not at the front, where there are lights and queues and all kinds of potential hassle, but at the scuffed grey doors of the emergency exit at the back. Rob steps out on to the street, nondescript in a black woolly hat and grey tracksuit, and follows Jonah up the dingy corridor to the emergency exit doors at the bottom of the cinema foyer. The twenty or so band and crew members who have signed up for the outing come behind in a loose pack. All the tickets have already been bought and Jonah leads them briskly up the side aisle in the gloom. Rob takes his seat at the back, with Marv right behind him. Jonah has now embarked on Operation Popcorn, pacing anonymously out to the front foyer and returning with a medium-sized box of Salted Without Butter. 'You're able to cover any eventuality,' says Jonah, 'by having people on standby to deal with the situation, so that the Principal is not affected in any way, shape or form. As far as they're concerned everything is normal. Everything is rosy and things flow.'

At midnight the bar of the Atlantic Kempinski is crowded with a noisy mix of crew and band (both are staying, in this city, at the same hotel). Claire's missing her fiancé Dylan; she phoned him in London and he was as out of it as she was. Tom has different preoccupations. 'Jesus, dude,' he complains. 'Fil gets to shag the girls, then I get the bloody e-mails.' The best looking of the Bird Alert trio has been in touch on a daily basis. Despite his heavy night last night, Fil's 'on the lash' again. He and Yolanda are laughing over a local newspaper, which contains an untranslatable piece headlined 'SEXY ROBBIE WILLIAMS'.

It's Yolanda's first European tour with the band, and a good one, she reckons. Not like some she's been on. She makes a face. 'Rob's management and the people he's hired as tour managers and so on are great. They're really nice people. Courteous, which is what you want.'

She first got into bass playing when she was about fourteen, having run through recorder, clarinet, trumpet and guitar at school before that. 'But I

started picking out the bass lines on the guitar –
that's the part of music that spoke to me. By fifteen
I'd made up my mind I liked the bass the most. It
took me a long time, didn't it?' she says, with that
engaging quaver in her voice.

She worked in Sainsbury's to save up for her first
guitar, then one of the little bands she was in got a bit
of profile and went on tour. She auditioned to be in
the band of a late-night Jonathan Ross pilot, which
never took off, but she met Paul Weller, who invited
her (she mimics him) 'to come along and have a jam,
girl'. So she joined his band for a bit, and by the time
she left, she was on her way.

Yolanda's only been with Robbie since last
September. She'd known Guy from his Lemon Trees
days (their drummer was a good mate of hers) and
she'd done a bit of work with him then, but hadn't
kept in contact. Then, last July, she got a call from his
office asking if she wanted a try-out with Rob; after
a jam with Guy, Gary and Chris she was asked to
join the band.

She'd never actually seen Rob perform before that.
'And I didn't really notice much of the press and
stuff, because I don't take much notice of the pop
press and television.' Guy thought it was a good thing
she came without expectations and wasn't in awe of
the star's reputation. 'He felt that I was actually quite
natural with Rob when I first met him. He was a
familiar face, but I was pretty kind of, "All right,
mate," rather than, "Oh, wow, it's Robbie Williams."'

'Yo,' muses Rob, with a smile, 'I had a shuffle, a cabinet reshuffle, and this lady came in. And from day one, just fitted straight in. She didn't miss a step. She just came in and it was, "Oh, there's Yolanda. It was like she's always been there. She looks amazing on stage."'

Life Disorder

'The majority of the fans, who sit in hotel lobbies, or outside hotels, or my house, are missing love in their real life. That's what I've come to believe.' It's the next morning and Rob's bus is moving off from the hotel, on the way to a football match with a local team of German techies, leaving the double row of fans behind, waving their autograph books at the darkened windows of the downstairs lounge. Rob can see them, but they can't see him.

'They are obviously missing some real love in some way; from their parents or boyfriends or from whoever has treated them badly. So they go and look into this love that's unobtainable – me. Or whoever the object may be. Delete me and put in Ronan Keating. Or Bono. Or whoever. A lot of them, I've noticed, are anorexic, bulimic, obese – you actually go and talk to them and they've all got some form of disorder, life disorder. They're immensely timid or immensely shy. Or just very young, yeah.

'There was this one that used to follow me all the time and she was very, very thin and she walked with a limp. She had this black hair. She used to be there

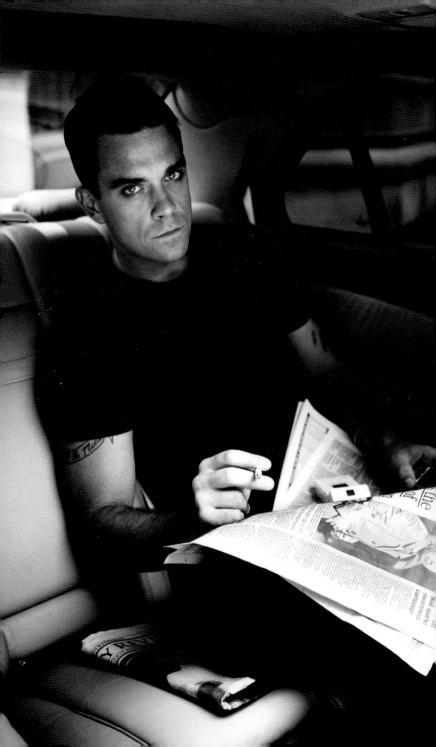

with Take That from the early days. And from day dot I couldn't stand the hysteria that was happening, these people coming in my space and staring at me, I couldn't stand it. You can't force yourself on someone, can you?'

He leans over to Chris and stares at him, his eyes transfixed and scary. Chris moves back, laughing the Scouser laugh. 'See!' says Rob, 'I've only been doing it for ten seconds.

'Anyway,' he continues, 'as my drinking progressed, or my drug taking progressed – if I was pissed I'd be angry and if I was hungover I'd be angry. Invariably I'd be these two things on a day-to-day basis, because of the stress of going on tour, of being whatever, so I'd drink on top of it. So if any fans got in my space I'd be quite abusive. I'd say, "Why are you still here? I haven't spoken to you for years. The only time I ever speak to you is to ask you to leave, so why do you keep coming back? It's not the action of a sane person to stay in the same room as somebody who doesn't want you there." Then they'd say, "Well, we put you where you are today." But when Mr Sainsbury, or whoever, started selling his products, nobody went and knocked on his door and asked for their money back because they bought apples from him. People buy my records because they like them, they come to see my show because they like it. But at the end of the day if they didn't like it they wouldn't come and they wouldn't buy it, so I don't owe anything to anybody.

'I see your picture,
she lives near me,

I went in her house
once, I was on TV,

Her boyfriend loves
me, I didn't care,

Because I got to smell
– her underwear.'

'Anyway, I'd just left Germany and I got to this hotel in Iceland and the phone goes and it's this girl, the one with the limp and the black hair. She said, "Hello." I said, "Hello." "Robbie," she said, "d'you know who this is?" I said, "I've got a feeling I know who it is." She said, "D'you know my name?" I said, "No." She said, "Oh, Robbie, I've been following you for seven years." I said, "Are you the girl with the black hair who walks with a limp?" She said, "Yes." I said, "No, I don't know your name." She said, "I've been following you for seven years and you do not know my name. I just want to tell you that I will not be following you any more." I said, "All right then." She said, "Is that it?" I said, "Yeah." I said, "To be honest with you …"

'And we had this discussion. For me, it came from love; it was a loving discussion. I said, "Look, what are you doing? How old are you now?" She was 27 or something. I said, "It's time to grow up and get your own life. You've been following me for ever and I've never even spoken to you. Only to shout at you." I said, "I don't know who you are and I don't want to know who you are. You say you want to be my friend. Friends don't come to hotel lobbies and sit there if I don't want them there. It's not how you get to be my friend and I'm sorry but we're not going to be friends." She said, "You're right." And I said, "Listen, look after yourself, but please, go and get a life. And I don't mean 'Go and get a life' with an exclamation mark, I genuinely mean that with love.

Go and get a life, because this is no life." '

The paradox is that it's hard for Rob to have real friends, these days; he can count them on the fingers of one hand. Jonathan Wilkes, his flatmate, who's known him all his life. A couple of girls in London, and men in LA, and that's it. 'I have acquaintances and a few mates, but I just don't have friends. It's sad for me. Take my best mate from school, Lee. Me and Johnny laugh, but Lee and I used to laugh and laugh and laugh. We spent a lot of time together growing up. Then I phoned him up once. I think this is when I gave up on everybody back home. I said, "Can I come round and see you?" He said, "Well, I need to clean the house and put my suit on." And then he was all embarrassed that his house was a mess. And it made me really sad. Because he just wouldn't have bothered in the old days. I go away for six months and become a pop star and you come back and it's Robbie Williams. You're not the same person any more.'

As Robbie Williams the pop star arrives at the football pitch in a nameless part of the Hamburg suburban sprawl, the press are already there, leaping out of cars, ready to get that crucial, ever-lucrative Robbie-shot. Marv and Jonah are immediately on the case, making plans to keep the paparazzi out of the ground altogether. But Rob wants to let them in. 'Let them take some photos, sell some records,' he tells his minders. No, he's not going to do an interview, but it's OK for them to be there. As long as they're kept to one side, away from the changing rooms. Anyway, he wants Marv, Jonah and Pompey, on the pitch, in his team.

So it's left to Josie to keep back the press. A small figure in a checked coat, she tries to corral them at one end of the boundary fence, away from the changing rooms, but they keep drifting back. 'Vy should ve?' asks one grumpy grey-haired character. 'Please can you keep over there?' she calls in vain. Another persistent blond journo in a black corduroy suit quizzes her keenly; she comes back laughing, imitating him.

'"Robbie iss a bick football fan? Of vich club?"'

'"Port Vale."'

'"I have never heard of zis."'

As the game gets underway it starts to drizzle, but the group of spectators gets ever larger. More photographers appear, running round the corner slung with cameras; one very determined pair marching up to a midfield perspective. Then, in ones and twos and threes, the girls crowd in, clutching umbrellas and coloured mobile phones, till there are well over a hundred, standing gawping at their idol in the Thursday morning rain. At this entirely private event, for which there was no publicity.

After the game, there's a recording session, in a studio in another remote part of town. Through a nondescript metal door, you clatter up tatty concrete steps to a waiting area with sofas, bowls of fruit on tables, a fridge full of soft drinks. In an inner room, by a huge console, Guy sits alongside a long-haired technician wearing patterned brown bedroom slippers. Yolanda, hair swept back in a bun, big sunglasses on top of her head, is slumped back on a sofa with drummer Chris. Through a glass screen Rob sits up on a stool at a mike in his silvery-grey tracksuit. Behind him a slowly revolving mirror-ball throws dots of coloured light in swirling patterns.

Gabby Chelmicka is here. She's flown out from London for a few nights to check on the tour. This is quite often what they do, she says, Guy and Rob – go to a studio mid-tour to get some stuff laid down.

'Rob's passion is writing songs, and it needs to be encouraged and stimulated, otherwise he goes mad with boredom. Rob's brain works really quickly. He finds it difficult to relax and sit in silence.'

As if on cue, Rob wanders in from the studio, holding a guitar. 'When's the food coming, Jose?' he says. He sits by the console, strums and sings softly. It's the song he came up with on the bus yesterday. 'Everybody's toxic in this town, I am a child and the child is feeling down…'

'Shall we put something rough down now?' says Guy. Rob heads back through to the studio and starts singing his lyric again.

'Ello ello ello,' goes Guy over the sound system.

'I just stand here and go Ello-lo-lo-lo-lo-oo,' jokes Rob, up on his stool at the big circular mike. He wanders over towards the mirror-ball. 'I'm going to have a piano like this in my new house,' he says, fingering the buffed gloss black surface.

'The one I've got in my house is a good size,' says Guy. 'Boudoir grand, it's called.'

Guy goes back through into the console room and they start work, Rob giving it his all.

'All God's children fade and die, In the name of "Let's get high". Ay-men! Then we do it again,' he sings.

Smoke rises from his discarded fag in the ashtray and curls around his tracksuited knee. He sings on, hands clenched tensely, jiggling up and down nervously on the stool. Guy plays it back to him with added beat. 'You've made it all work,' he tells his collaborator, 'haven't you? You're really great for that.'

Josie brings a plate of food through.

'Can I eat now?' Rob asks. 'Cos I'm getting hungry.' In his muted Stoke accent it sounds like 'angry'. He takes his plate and leaves the studio. Guy goes in and plays piano over the stuff that Rob has recorded. Rob finishes his meal and lets out a loud, long burp.

'Nott batt!' laughs the German technician at his console.

Rob returns to the studio and gets back to it, Guy nodding encouragement through the glass screen, conducting him with a finger.

'I want to cry, but I don't make a sound, I am your child and your child is feeling do-o-own,' goes Rob.

He breaks off.

'What d'you think?' asks Guy gently.

'It's just the words.'

'Yeah. Shall we forget them for now?'

'D'you think it's a bit pants?'

'I'm not sure. I think it needs to be something pretty shouty, d'you know what I mean? We can do it another day. It needs to be something really aggressive, I think. Quite Limp Bizkit-esque. Quite Fred Dursk-esque.'

Yolanda is laughing. 'Chilli Peppers-esque,' she says.

'He doesn't shout,' says Rob.

'They all shout in America,' says Guy.

'They do, don't they?'

'Make themselves heard.'

'America,' muses Rob. 'If I lived there I'd shout.'

And so they go on, chattering inconsequentially between jams. 'Sticks and stones may break my bones,' croons Rob. 'Words can burn a happy home. It's true. I've got words for you – hic.'

Oh dear. Rob's got hiccoughs.

'You need a nasty shock,' says Guy. 'That's what my mother used to say when I was younger.'

'Then we do it again – hic,' goes Rob. 'Everybody's toxic in this – hic.'

They abandon Tox-hic in favour of a new song. 'Haf you a name for it?' asks the German technician.

'Call it "Total Bollocks, Part One",' says Guy. He must have guessed what's coming. The outer studio is filled with music as Rob, Guy and Yolanda jam away together, Rob improvising words to fit the sound. 'Move, move, move, OK… I see your picture and I get high… I see your picture, I want to die. Going to groove, groove, groove, girl on me… Going to lay your clothes around me… why don't you live, live, live with me.' Amid the semi-comprehensible gibberish, only, 'I see your picture and I get high,' emerges clearly. Then suddenly, 'I love LA.' Rob stops abruptly.

Then another tune, another lyric has intruded. 'I love you, baby, but she's the one. I see your picture…' There is more incomprehensible moan-singing from Rob. You can only make out individual phrases: 'I'll be your dad… She touches places that I never… She's the finest…'. 'I love you, baby, but she's the one,' keeps returning, then suddenly there's a clutch of lyric.

> I see your picture, she lives near me,
> I went in her house once, I was on TV,
> Her boyfriend loves me, I didn't care,
> Because I got to smell – her underwear.

'That was good, that verse that I sang,' says Rob, after a bit. They decide to tape it. The underwear theme stays, even as the other words change. The boyfriend becomes husband becomes fella, 'he loves her, he's gonna tell her, she knows I'm watching, and so's her fella, I'll keep on watching, and fuck her fella…'

'Quite good, really,' says Guy, when they break. Ever-enthusiastic David likes it too, but now they've got to go, off to their self-help meeting. Rob might go down to the Reeperbahn later, with Franksy. 'I want to see how much it disgusts me,' he says, 'and turns me on in a strange kind of way as well.' Outside the studio the Hamburg girls' network has already tracked down their idol. There's maybe fifteen of them by the back door with cameras and autograph books. Plus a few blokes, too.

Gabby laughs as we get on the bus to go back to the hotel. The girls want to shag him and the guys want to be him. He's the Sinatra of his time, though last night he was saying he felt, with a film crew watching him the whole time, like the subject of one of those David Attenborough wildlife specials.

On his second visit in a row to the deeply delicious Italian restaurant run by the German-speaking Indian, Fil orders exactly the same starter and main course. He might not be sentimental about girls but he clearly is about food.

'Well, when you're on tour sex is something different. It's a laugh, and there's this locker-room humour that goes with it. Everybody on the bus the next day goes, "Waah! Fil got a shag. Come on, tell us about it," or whatever.

'Maybe it's all part of performing. The whole thing is just an ego trip. Get on stage, you get some attention, you come off feeling like a million quid and you think, This is great. I must have a shag and capitalise on one's success. It's like the drugs and the booze and all the rest of it, it's all for that reason. The trouble is, these things spill over into your – I wouldn't say normal life – your other life. There's my touring life, then there's my home life – and the edges start getting a bit blurred. You get home,' he laughs, 'and you start calling room service, dialling nine for an outside line.'

Fil's just come out of a long relationship, and to be honest he doesn't get the whole serial monogamy thing. He looks at all his friends doing it. 'And I think, How can you possibly have fallen in love so many times and been with so many people? I can't think of anything worse than having to spend all your time with someone who doesn't really do it for you. What's the point of that?'

Over a second bottle of quite pricey Chianti (but what the hell, he's just got a great publishing deal), Fil suddenly opens up. About his Czech background; growing up in Prague; how his psychologist father had escaped with the family to England when Fil was eight; how their little Fiat 127 with all their belongings stashed on the top got ripped apart at the border. Fil's folks had some hard currency hidden in a vase, 'which was covered in scrunched-up bits of newspaper and stuff. And this border guard who was searching the car had his hand right in it. If he'd found that, we'd have got sent straight back, but he kind of rummaged around in there for a while and then took his hand out – so we got through.' But then, when they'd finally arrived in Dover three days later, in the middle of a blizzard, this car skidded past them, smashed into a cliff, and nearly wiped them out the second they actually set foot in Britain…

Settling in Forest Hill, South London, things got worse, as the young Beatles-loving Czech boy found himself having the shit kicked out of him because he couldn't speak English. 'That changed pretty quick,' he says now. 'Kids pick things up quick if they're thrown in the deep end like that – I could speak good English within six months. But I was still the whipping post for them.'

Fil's father had taught him to play the guitar when he was eight or nine. 'I knew I was good, man. That's not to be arrogant or anything. It was the one thing I had left to cling to, because the rest of my life was misery. I used to bunk off every lesson I could and go and play guitar.'

Eventually Fil ended up helping with the guitar lessons in the school. 'One of the young kids heard me and said to a bloke in the room, who'd been playing guitar for ages, "That Eisler's good. D'you think he's going to make it?" And this older guy said, right in front of me, "No chance. He's not going to amount to anything. Because it's too hard. It's not going to happen to you. Get used to that idea. Learn something else. Yeah, you're an all right guitar player, but you're not going to make it. Look at me."

'But here's the beautiful pay-off.' Fil grins. Many

years later, when he'd served his apprenticeship, played in crappy venues, been in his embarrassing prog-rock band (Nexus), practised eight hours a day, not had the patience to go to music college, been phoned by Guy, whom he'd met doing a gig with Zoe, the 'Sunshine On A Rainy Day' woman, joined the Robbie band, been a part of it as Rob took off as a solo artist, played Slane Castle etc., he was walking past a pub and he saw a sign with this guy's name on it, advertising a Christmas Eve gig. 'I thought, it can't be. So I walked in. I thought, I've got to go and check this out. I said, "You've got to show me a flyer. Is there a picture of this geezer?" The landlady went, "Yeah, sure," and gets this poster out. Bang. It's him. I was like, Yessss! Sadly I was away on Christmas Eve. Otherwise I would have dropped my plans and turned up. But I left him a note instead, and it was something along the lines of, "I don't know if you remember me, but I'm the kid you said would amount to absolutely nothing. I did amount to absolutely fuck all, just recently, in front of half a million people at Slane Castle. Have a good show. Ta ta." Something along those lines – and it felt very, very good indeed, actually.'

For Rob, of course, success brings problems as well as rewards. Back at the hotel the bar is full of band and crew and the lobby is crowded with fans again. He actually came down to the bar earlier, says twenty-year-old Bine, who has booked into a room with three girlfriends upstairs. But unfortunately he turned round and went straight back into the lift again.

'I came down for two minutes,' Rob says, 'and the whole place converged on me. The fans' eyes came to me and didn't come off me. Four or five people came up to me in the first two minutes that I was there. They've got courage from the drink and a feeling that they own you in some way. So it's time for me to turn tail and go back up to my room. I can't sit in that. I don't know how people do it. Otherwise they just stare at you and follow you around all night. Even if they don't come up and say anything, if you've got a group of twenty people wherever you are, you don't want to leave your room, do you?'

5

'There is this huge
devil inside me. And
it doesn't come out
and act out against
other people; it just
wants me to destroy
myself. I have a disease
that talks to me in my
own voice and tells me
I haven't got it. And
that's my dark side.'

TRYING TO FIND ROBERT

There was a reason why there were quite so many fans in the hotel last night, Rob says, as he sits in his dressing room before the Hamburg gig, naked to the waist. After he and David had left the recording studio, he was followed by the press, who had tracked him from the football to the studio and then on to his self-help meeting.

'We got into a smaller vehicle and managed to leave a lot of them behind, but there was this one persistent guy from Radio Hamburg, who pulled up right outside the meeting. I thought, What am I going to do now? So I went up to the car and sat down and did the nicest me that I do. Which is, Look, I'm coming from a sincere place and this is me asking you very kindly. I sat down with him and said, "Look, mate, how are you?" I shook his hand. And I said, "I'm just about to go and do something that's very personal now. I'd appreciate it if you didn't follow me." And he went, "Sure. As long as you can tell me where I can meet you later." Now in the long run I should have gone, "OK, cool. I'll tell you what we'll do. I've got half an hour tonight at eleven o'clock." And then I would have gone, "Piss off." That's what I should have done. But I just looked at him and I said, "This isn't open to conditions. It's not a bribe." He'd got his recording equipment, his microphone and his mini disc right there and the recording light was on. I thought, What am I going to do here? He looked at me and said, "You tell me why I should not follow you?" I looked down at his recording equipment and his phone rang. As his phone rang I reached into the car, grabbed his equipment, pulled the microphone out of its socket, threw the mini disc away, got the microphone, flung it into a tree and walked off.

'I walked off to the meeting with the blood of anger running. I thought, I've just poured my heart out to you and you're still treating me like I'm worthless. Like my feelings don't mean anything to you whatsoever. You intend to hurt me. And that makes me scared, which in turn makes me angry.

'We went to the meeting and when I came out of the building there's four police there and I would say about fifteen other people. And what he'd done while I was in the meeting was he'd got his mobile phone live on the radio and told Hamburg what I was doing. And that was why everyone had come. So I'd just gone into this safe place and walked out into this mad world of Robbie. I got in the car and I said, "Marv, what did the police say to you?" The police had told the fellow from Radio Hamburg to piss off basically. And Marv went and found his stuff for him and gave it back to him and told him to piss off, too.

'I walked off with the blood of anger running. I thought, I've just poured my heart out to you and you're still treating me like I'm worthless.'

'It's comical. When I got back to the hotel it was funny. But as it was happening it wasn't. People like that are some kind of scum.'

A Little Oasis

'We've done tours dry before,' says David Enthoven, 'but this time, for the first time, I would say Rob's made a decision really for himself. Maybe before, he hadn't quite thrown the towel in. This time I really think he has. He's extremely vulnerable. And with the best will in the world, I don't know anybody else – how many months is he now, two months sober? – who could possibly go out and actually be at his best. The last thing you want to do is be standing in front of 10,000 people and trying to entertain them. All you really want to be doing is going to a meeting or talking to me about it or talking to other people who are fighting all this fear, rather than having to go out and be this person, this entertainer – Robbie.

'He's trying to find Robert, but then he's having to go out and be Robbie. That's the dichotomy of the thing.'

David is revealingly honest as he elaborates on what he does for Rob. 'My job on the road is pretty simple, really. I have to prepare Rob to be in the best frame of mind possible to get out and do his job. His job is to put smiles on 10,000 to 15,000 people's faces every night. So I spend a lot of time with him. We know what my role is. He quite often pulls my leg and says, "David, your job is to get me to feel right." So it's a lot of affirmation. I think it takes tremendous courage to do what he's doing in the condition he's in. I suppose my job is to actually help him with that courage or actually put him in the right frame of mind. But at the end of the day it's still down to that lad to actually go out and do it.'

'These self-help meetings are an essential part of the tour, aren't they?'

'Yeah, they are. We go and find these little oases, basically. We go to some good meetings and some bad meetings, but it's quite good to get away from the tour and just go and meet normal Belgian and German people, English-speaking or whatever, suffering from the same problem. There is a sharing of strengths. You actually talk about how it is and what's going on for you. The great thing about these meetings is, you walk in there and you know everybody in that room has got the same problem as you. They have actually acknowledged the fact "Enough's enough" and they are trying to get through the day without having a drink.'

Really Cool and Mean

David's interest in Rob remaining clean is more than just professional. His own life having been scarred, one might almost say defined, by drink and drugs, this is not a subject to be taken lightly. From his earliest days in the music business he had used them regularly. By the seventies, with a string of rock legends on his management CV, David was, in his own words, 'The coolest kid on the block. I had the Easy Rider bike, up and down the King's Road. I was rock 'n' roll's frigging answer to…' He shakes his head, breaking into gurgling laughter at the absurdity of his younger self. 'Everybody would say, "Yeah, David's really cool and mean" and all the rest of it. And I was this terrified little boy inside. The only way he could be cool was when he was high as a kite.

'I could always stop,' he goes on. 'There was never any problem about stopping. I was very strong like that. I could stop for three or four days, a month sometimes. But I always got bored and started again. I used to get clean and think, Now what? Then I'd get invaded with all these feelings of inadequacy, low self-esteem. Couldn't deal with that. "Let's have some more!" And try to kill all the internal feeling.'

By 1977 his drugs habit had increased to a level beyond the recreational. He was asked by his partners to leave EG, the hugely successful management outfit he'd help found. 'I was becoming pretty erratic. Too much cocaine and various substances.' His descent from there was, 'All very messy, to be honest with you. I didn't handle things well.' David lost his marriage, his two children, his big house in the country, his collection of 43 motorbikes, and 'a huge amount of money, which I went and blew in a complete drug-crazed binge, basically'. He ended up sleeping in a room down on the south coast, by now a full-blown heroin and cocaine addict. 'Blaming,

blaming, blaming everybody really, but not looking at myself to realise that it was me who had to get myself together.'

Finally he reached the bottom of the pit. Over Christmas 1985 he thought seriously about killing himself. 'And I realised it was a pretty good option. I was doing speed and alcohol again, which is a horrible combination. I had nowhere to go. My children didn't want me. My friends didn't want me. My mother was dead. I was living in the place she'd lived in with all her clothes around. It was mad. Living in her bed with my two dogs.'

In desperation, he called an ex-alcoholic friend and went into rehab in January 1986, at Broadway Lodge in Weston-super-Mare. He stayed ten weeks. 'I never want to do that again. It terrified me. I remember getting to the station afterwards and just looking up and seeing an advert for a bottle of brandy and thinking, Oh God, that would do the trick. Then I thought, Do the trick, you silly arse. You've just spent ten weeks in hell. D'you want to go through all that all over again?'

So he stayed clean, and crawled back to normality. 'Tim will tell you what state I was in. He came to see me at the treatment centre, bless him. He brought me some cigarettes. When I was pitching myself around the music industry again trying to get a job, I literally couldn't look people in the eye.'

David moved into bedsit land, knocking on doors selling 'perfumes that smelt like other perfumes'. But deep down he was still determined 'to be the one thing I wanted and knew I was good at'.

One night, sitting in a bedsit in Parsons Green, 'heading back towards Chelsea, where I definitely felt I belonged', David had a revelation. 'I was in this tiny room, with my old school trunk. It was in this very sweet woman's house, and I'd just paid her £75 for the rent. And I'd got £75 in my pocket. All my possessions basically were in that room, which was nothing, because I'd burnt everything, all my suits and everything. And I must have been about two and a half years clean. And I was thinking, Yeah, this is OK. I was happy'.

David was 44. He decided he was going to go back into music, give it another go. He moved in with his future wife, Maren, who, he says 'gave me the strength to go out into the world'.

'I went round the record companies asking, "Has anybody got a band?"'

He got started with a group called The Grid. Then Bryan Ferry heard he was back in business and gave him a call, which gave him 'the shop window to get going properly'. Then he offered Tim Clark some space in his office and the two old pals 'started dabbling in little musical projects'. Then Massive Attack were recommended to them. 'That set us up, really. Bryan was old and cool, but Massive were young and cool.' And then a call from one of Bryan Ferry's accountants brought in Robbie Williams.

'I've never seen myself as the boss, I always see myself as the bloke at the front. The big difference is I get paid more.

The crew have always been so nice to me that it's like a group effort. It's not me and them or them and him.

I know they regard me with respect, and they know I'm the man that pays the wages, but I don't think any of them are scared of me.

I think they all genuinely like me.'

Living with Robbie

Richie Stevenson, the front-of-house merchandising salesman, is in a state of high nervousness. He didn't turn up to the football on Wednesday, which is a pretty serious offence in tour terms. And now everyone's been really off with him all day. He understands why, because he let everyone down, but it wasn't his fault... Even Rob's been different. 'I think you're going to have to have a word with Franksy later,' he says, coldly, when he sees Richie.

For three and a half hours, Richie's on the rack. Every possible scenario's going through his head. Now Claire's turned up at his stall, wanting her free allocation of merchandise, just in case he's not there tomorrow. Little Jez and Adam Birch, Fil's guitar-tech, stop to hug him, as if it's his last day.

Then an hour before the gig, Franksy gets the trembling merchandise salesman into Rob's dressing room. 'Sit down,' Rob says. He's signing a stack of autographs for Josie, not meeting Richie's eye.

'You didn't turn up to football on Wednesday, did you?'

'No,' says Richie. He doesn't want to explain that his van was boxed in, because that sounds like too much of a lame excuse, so he sits quietly. Rob's face is a picture of seriousness as he continues his signing.

'I've decided to –' Rob says, then stalls. Richie's ready for the worst. The long trip home to Sheffield, the end of a career that has given him a deep famil-iarity with every foyer in Europe. 'I've decided to...

wind you up all day.'

While they're all laughing, Rob hugs him. Richie's relief is immense. 'Thanks, cheers for that,' he's muttering.

'I think you'd best leave while you're ahead,' says Franksy. The Prince of Darkness was originally looking at the full three-day wind-up, 'so you have a night to think about it.' But he and Rob relented.

The Stage Mix

Up in the little stage-left area, his tall frame hunched slightly as he bends over, glasses gleaming, Canadian monitor engineer Martin Wareing moves his hands expertly over the endless rows of coloured dials that mix not the music the audience hear but the sound for each of the individual members of the band to listen to and play from, which comes from individual monitors in front of their places on stage. 'So Fil, for example, likes to hear lots of drums, kicking snare and stuff, and he uses that to keep his timing and things. Guy obviously needs to hear his keyboards really well, and then he likes a mix of vocals and Claire's keyboards too. Because he's so close to Chris on stage, he doesn't need to hear too much drums.

'But for 70 per cent of the show, I'm listening to what Rob's doing.' As Rob races around the stage, Martin keeps the right sound following him for his best possible performance. 'He's pretty much every-where. Those two monitors you can see at the centre of the stage are pretty much just for Rob.'

Behind the Canadian, chewing gum impassively in the darkness, is his 'babysitter' Dave 'Dribble' Poynter, ready to take over if Martin has to run on stage or leave for any other reason. 'I'm called Dribble because I dribble a lot,' Dave explains, without any apparent embarrassment.

Now, on this fourth gig of the tour, the details of Robbie's performance are starting to become familiar. The way he clutches his mike stand during 'Beautiful Day'. The way he shakes his head to the right during 'The Road To Mandalay'; the way he swaggers down the stage during 'Forever Texas' – 'Pretty la-ady, am-aze me'; then fixes on someone in the audience and does something sexual, tonight pulling one finger in and out of his mouth, slowly, back and forth, so suggestively, then raises his eyebrows and walks off, leaving the girls visibly gasping; the way he smokes during 'No Regrets', striding, yes, indeed, Sinatra-like, to the end of the stage; the way he jumps up like a kid during 'Paint By Numbers'; his little riff at the start of 'Supreme'. 'You – don't – want-to-fuck-with-Robbie. Cause Rob-bie – will fucking-kill-you.' 'I'm a bad man,' he adds tonight.

There are some other new touches, too. When he asks the ladies – during 'Forever Texas' – to get their tits out, it's in German, 'Zeigt mir eure Titten', which raises a huge laugh. There's another joke too, which has also been printed out in big capitals by Wob on Rob's front-stage monitor. Somebody at the hotel, he tells the crowd, told him to say, 'Alles fit im Schritt?' if he wanted to ask them how they're doing. But of course it doesn't mean 'How're you doing?' at all. 'Is everything OK between your legs?' is the nearest translation to it. The crowd roars with the excitement of young people who know their parents would be shocked were they here.

And tonight Gary has some fans: three girls holding up little bobbing squares of cardboard reading G, A, R and Y. 'What you don't know,' Rob tells Gary on stage, 'is they've got Gary Barlow over there. I used to be in a band called Take That,' he explains, never overestimating his audience.

After the show Stephanie, Zena and Maria linger by the stage. Why do they like Gary so much?

'He's kind.'

So if they were allowed to spend the rest of their lives with either Gary or Robbie, who would they choose?

The trio squeak with laughter. 'I think there's more time for living with Robbie,' says Zena, practically. 'I mean, because Gary's older.'

'I would take Guy,' says Stephanie. 'But he's just married.'

Don't they have boyfriends?

'Oh yes.'

And what do they think?

'They hate it.'

B-Side

Rob emerges from the lift of the Atlantic Kempinski in dark glasses and a bright green woolly hat. Though you can't see his eyes, you can see him scanning the entire foyer, taking everything in. Then, with Jonah hovering a yard behind, hands hanging down semi-taut, ready for action, Rob's off and out through the revolving doors and the gauntlet of fans to his bus, his regular posse of David and Josie following. 'Robbie, Robbie!' they shout, holding up autograph books, but he's not signing anything today, he tells them, pausing mid-pavement in the sunshine. 'Listen, have a very good day. Go and get some warmth. No,' he reiterates to one desperate fan, 'if I sign one, I'll have to sign everybody's.' He smiles broadly. 'You take care. See you later.'

The band follows. Claire's carrying the bunch of roses that fiancé Dylan sent her for Valentine's Day. 'Every rose he's ever given me, I've kept,' she says, with a semi-apologetic grin. It sounds like a line from a Robbie lyric. Fil, meanwhile, has been sent a press clipping from an English tabloid, featuring him and Robbie in a close clinch: 'FIL'S GOT A HOBBY', it reads, 'HE LOVES SHAGGING ROBBIE'. He's not happy, he says, as he shows it round.

Gary Nuttall takes his regular seat next to Morris the driver – he suffers from travel sickness, so always sits at the front of the bus. He's been enjoying

Hamburg. Just walking around, looking in a few shops. 'Not those kinds of shops,' he laughs. But he loves the seediness of it all, the Reeperbahn and all of that. 'Because of the Beatles connection. John Lennon always said the best of the Beatles music was when they were in Germany.'

Gary first got into music when Elvis died, in 1977. He was eleven. 'And I just became fascinated with this guy.' The first song he ever learnt on the guitar was 'Wooden Heart' – 'a really old, easy Elvis track' and he was soon playing working men's clubs. Around the age of eighteen, he entered his pub-band phase. No longer doing covers, but original songs, in bands whose names he can't even remember. Then the drummer with Face – Gary's second 'proper band' – got called up to do an audition for Robbie Williams. He got the job and phoned Gary up, saying they needed a guitarist. 'The funny thing is, going back to my liking for bed, one of my best mates always used to say to me, "You'll never get anywhere, Gary, if you're lying in bed all day." But Smiley phoned me at 3.30 in the afternoon and I was in bed. If I'd been out looking for work I'd never have got the phone call.'

Guy and Fil went to watch him play at the Borderline and he was signed up. So he was in the Robbie Williams band, all of them dressed in white suits for TFI Friday. It was great to have some money for a change, but Gary doubted it would last a year.

'One of the first things Rob said to me, actually,

when I joined – and I got on with Rob straight away, I had an instant thing with him, I love him, he's great – he said to me, "Look, Gary, I won't kid you, if this doesn't take off or nothing happens, I'm not one of those people that's going to run it into the ground or keep on trying. If it doesn't work, that's it." That was his attitude. If it wasn't working, he'd just go off and do something else.'

Then they released 'Angels'. 'We were in the back of the car and I remember Rob saying, "When I hear songs like that I think everything's going to be all right." And when it came out, it got in the Top 10 and I thought, It's going to go on for a bit longer. But then it all took off. It was amazing. For Rob, it's an immense pressure and I can't get my head around what that must be like, to be at the centre of all that attention, but for someone like me it's great to be around it and see what's going on. To be kind of at the centre of it and still be able to go out and have a little walk around. No-one knows who you are. That's the best thing about it.'

It's all happened so fast. Gary can remember Rob's first ever solo gig, in 1997, at the Peacock Centre in Woking, a big room that holds two thousand, and it wasn't even half full. 'I always think back to that when we're doing Slane Castle or these stadium things. You think, How did this happen? I was always hoping something incredible would happen, because Rob's so good. I'm not just saying that. He's an expert. With the audience. Very charismatic. Even when he's out of it and at his worst – what he thinks of as his worst moments – he's great.'

Generous too, Gary thinks. Rob gave him the B-side of 'Lazy Days' for one of his own songs: '"She Makes Me High". I thought, Here's someone that's quite a giving sort of guy. He doesn't care who he does his stuff with. It's not as precious as some people make it out to be. He's very open about it.

'I remember when that came out. Me and the girlfriend were going round each shop looking at the CD, looking at the back and looking at my name. "Yeah, it's on that one."' He chuckles at the memory. 'It was a buzz. And it really does help me out, because he's one of the biggest singers in the country.'

So what about his fans?

Gary laughs his breathless, slightly high-pitched laugh. The trouble is, he can't see them, because he takes his glasses off to perform, and the front row becomes a bit of a blur. 'We get out of the bus and Rob goes straight past them. I always tend to say, "How are you? Are you all right? Have you seen him yet?" Stop and say hello. Because I think they're out there and it's freezing and it's like, at least someone has said hello to them.'

His fans are right: Gary is kind.

6

'I don't know what
I look for in a woman.
I'm not looking.

I'm sticking to men.'

ROCK 'N' ROLL VETERAN

The hotel is in the old east side of Berlin, it transpires. In the brilliant Monday morning sunshine the figures walking up and down Charlottenstrasse are inky silhouettes against a dazzling pavement. Tim Clark has flown in for the Berlin gig; he and David stroll out down the broad streets in search of a coffee bar, veteran rock 'n' roll figures in heavy coats.

Tim is the other half of the 'double-headed' IE team, the one who stays behind in London managing the bigger picture while David is on the road with the artist. He's leaner than David is and more tanned and weather-beaten (as befits his upbringing in the Kenyan bush, where he dreamed of being a novelist). As he looks at you keenly over the unframed rectangular glasses that perch on the end of his nose, you imagine he drives a hard bargain, would do for the business side of things what David clearly does for the people side. Together, they're a relaxed team, joshing each other constantly, with the easy intimacy of very old mates.

They've known each other since 1968, when David signed King Crimson to Island Records. Tim had been working at Island since the end of '64, when he joined 'as a humble store man'. It was an extraordinarily exciting place to be, he remembers, even though at first 'all we had was Jamaican music, a little American R & B label and some rugby songs'. But then Island had a hit with Millie's 'My Boy Lollipop' and The Spencer Davis Group's 'Keep On Running' and they could start recording bands from the underground scene – Steve Winwood's Traffic, Free, Spooky Tooth, Jethro Tull and Mott the Hoople. 'It was great,' David agrees. 'I remember riding up to Neasden on my motorbike and you walked into this room and there were boxes of records everywhere. Complete chaos going on, but it was a real vibe, because all the records they were selling were cool. We'd got King Crimson away from Decca, which was this corporate building down on the Thames, the whole place built on Mantovani, who got about a farthing a record…'

In 1972, Tim was responsible for signing Roxy Music to Island 'in the teeth of great opposition from just about everybody' and along came Cat Stevens, ELP and Bad Company all of whom Tim worked with closely. 'We had all the coolest underground bands,' Tim remembers, 'as well as the folkies.' Fairport Convention, Nick Drake, John Martyn, the Thompsons. Then, as Tim became marketing director, Bob Marley was signed.

It was an exciting period for Island, for David's management group EG, and for their joint attitude to the creative work they were promoting. 'The great thing for me about Tim,' says David, 'was that he actually shared the artist's vision. That the record sleeves were not a corporate identity, they were more about trying to explain what the artists were about…'

It's a philosophy the two managers regard as central to their operation today, long after the changes of the late seventies and eighties, when Tim watched the early independent labels, Island included, sell out to the major record companies. 'I guess David and I are the two left who still believe in the ideals of the sixties, which is more power to the artist, simply put. I think in one sense, we're kind of enablers. The artists have a vision and we help them realise it.'

'And probably you'd be better at making Rob's vision come true than somebody of 27?'

'Oh yeah. That is something at the door of experience. David and I, in our separate ways, have done everything that one could possibly do in this industry short of being an artist or producer, a creator in the musical sense. We've been store man, roadie, up to Managing Director. We've negotiated record contracts from different sides of the table, from a record company perspective and from artists' perspectives. So the wool can't be pulled over our eyes.'

It's important that they're able to give Rob the creative freedom to do what he wants. 'We think there's nothing,' stresses Tim, 'without the artist and the musicians, these eccentric, hugely talented people that refuse to be packaged. There's no way Rob has been packaged by his record company, nothing could be further from the truth. Rob's created the way he wants to look.'

'EMI's idea,' laughs David, 'was, "Let's make him this good-looking young man." And all he does is show his arse. So he's given them the arse really.'

Crowding the corridor

'Welcome to the world of water,' says Rob, with a smile. To the left of the little corridor from the door there's a group of armchairs around a low coffee table. A sideboard laden with Evian, Coke and other soft drinks stands against the wall. Rob seems thoroughly relaxed tonight. But he didn't enjoy the Berlin gig, he says, didn't think it was as good as Hamburg.

He and David are already engaged in a fast Uno two-hander, throwing down the Action, Reverse and Skip cards in their well-worn routine. 'I thank you,' says Rob as he wins a round. Eventually David is out and Josie and Marv join in. Josie's laughing because some fan outside was hassling Franksy for an idea of where Robb-ieeeee was going next. 'Oh ple-e-e-ease,' she begged, 'can you give us a tip?' 'Don't wipe your arse with a broken bottle,' was Franksy's growled reply.

Rob, ever bright and restless, hurries the game along, calling out your name if you're more than a second behind the hand. 'David!' 'Mark!' 'Marv!'

There's a wanting-to-be-kind, Better Man side of him, but he's still the prince. 'Open that window for me, would you, David?' he asks. At other times he breaks off, to sing snatches of his own songs. Then he suddenly looks round at you and smiles, for no discernible reason.

A little later we're joshing around. I'm telling David and Josie that they remind me, as they stand on the edge of the stage night after night, dancing along to Rob's songs, of characters in Winnie the Pooh. Big bald David, in his loose Nelson Mandela style shirt, comparatively tiny Josie beside him – they're Pooh and Piglet (though I don't say that now).

'And me?' asks Rob.

'No, you're more Jungle Book.'

'What am I? A troubled gibbon.' He laughs loudly.

It's two in the morning but there are still some fans in the downstairs bar. Drinking tea at a table by the door are Marlene and Haydee, from Rostok on the Black Sea. Marlene, with a ginger mop and almond eyes, is a student. Her friend in black, with long dark hair and a big, strangely mobile mouth, has finished school and is waiting to go to university. They were both in the front row at the gig, Haydee standing out from the crowd with her Draculine good looks. Face to face, they are not just dumb beauties; they both have good English and are bright and articulate. They were only young when the wall came down, they tell me, so don't remember much about the old East Germany. But it wasn't so bad in the old days, Haydee insists. Everyone had a job.

Suddenly Jonah has appeared. He raises his eyebrows at me (I'd said I was going to bed) and starts offering drinks all round. But the girls are driving back to Rostok tonight, so they're only having tea. 'Keep that chair for me,' says Jonah.

When he sits down the conversation becomes altogether more stilted. 'How many men have you got in your cellar?' he asks Haydee. She giggles and looks rapidly between her friend and me. Is this supposed to be a joke, a chat-up line, or what?

After a few minutes of this, Jonah's mobile rings. He gets up and steps outside. He comes back in and sits down, a broad, slightly nervous smile under his moustache. 'D'you like cards?' he asks them. There's a card game going on upstairs and they want one more player. But only one. Would Haydee perhaps be interested?

Haydee giggles fetchingly. No, no, she's quite happy down here with her friend, she says. Jonah's concerned that she's not quite getting his drift. The person he works for would like to play Uno with her.

Haydee laughs. 'Oh no, I don't think I want to play Uno. It's a kids' game, isn't it?' she says.

'You don't have to play Uno,' says Jonah. 'Are they stupid?' he mutters under his breath, as his mobile rings again. This time the conversation round the corner is both more hushed and more earnest. The girls fully understand what's on offer. They wouldn't mind going up to meet Robbie, but Haydee doesn't want to go alone with Jonah.

He reappears, still on the phone. He's telling whoever's on the other end that he will be back shortly. 'Accompanied,' he says heavily.

A minute later and Marv appears. He's altogether more direct. 'You know who we work for, don't you?' he says. This person would be very happy to see Haydee in his room.

'This person,' adds Jonah, 'is someone whose gig you've recently been to see.' He nods meaningfully.

'Oh,' says Haydee with a laugh. 'Michael Jackson!'

The two security men exchange exasperated looks, then Jonah turns his biggest smile back on Haydee. Look, why doesn't she just come up and see who they're talking about. They can both go, and then one can stay and play cards and the other can come with them. Him and his colleague.

The girls are not going to be split up and even together they're not going anywhere with Marv and Jonah. 'We'd go up with you,' they say, turning to me. And foolishly, liking and feeling concerned for them, I agree.

We go up in the lift, an awkward fivesome. Along the corridor, Jonah knocks on Rob's door. A muffled 'come in' and Jonah ushers us through. Rob is there, alone, at the end of the short corridor into the main suite. He sees us, a crowd of people he hasn't asked for, and is suddenly freaked out.

'I have gushing praise
for all of my band.

I hate it when I read
that sort of stuff
about "my dancers"
or "my band" – but
it's the truth.

I love 'em.'

'I'm sorry,' he mutters, 'too many people.'

But he doesn't scream at us, he's polite as ever.

'Good night,' he adds.

We back out and troop down to the bar. When the girls have left, Jonah is philosophical. It was a fuck-up, basically. But you learn in these situations to pick yourself up, dust yourself down and carry on for another day.

A little later Marv appears. It's OK, he says. He's been talking to Rob about it and the boss thought it was quite funny.

It's a bizarre situation, being a young man trapped in a hotel room with hordes of dolled-up young women waiting for you in the lobby below. Not all of them want to progress beyond the game of cards, but plenty do. Rob can't come down and chat and flirt normally (and find out exactly who wants what) because he'd be overrun, so quite often he leaves the business of making the introductions to his trusted entourage.

One of Those Days

While the crew and band have done the eight-and-a-half-hour journey to Dusseldorf overnight by road, the Principal and management are flying. Two shiny black cars await Rob in the echoing concrete garage below the hotel. We're sped to the airport and led straight out to the departure lounge.

Rob doesn't seem too bothered by last night's incident. '*She's* pretty,' he says, as the pert blonde hostess heads back to the cabin. Then: 'I've been in my room for days,' he says in a lilting Elvis voice. 'For over a week now,' he adds in his normal voice. 'If I haven't been in my room I've been in a coach and if I haven't been in a coach I've been in a plane. And it can get a bit…'

'Stir-crazy?'

'Yeah. You know, if I go into my head alone, which I do invariably on many occasions, it's not a nice place, my head, alone… because of the thought patterns. Sometimes I just have to keep constantly fending off bad thoughts…'

He picks up a book and reads, every now and then looking up to gaze moodily out of the window.

It's not a good day. As we arrive at the Dusseldorf hotel, there's a posse of press waiting. As Rob walks in, the hotel manager comes to greet him. Before he knows it he's in a bit of a situation. 'It was a balding old chap in one of those suits that must be handed out to every hotel manager in the world. He grabs me by the hand. And as I go to shake his hand to say hello he tries to guide my arm so my body will open up to all of the press that are in a line behind. He physically tries to turn me round to get a picture of me and him to be in the papers. And that's no way to treat a guest of a hotel. You go to a hotel for privacy and that's what I go to a hotel for.'

Rob instantly demands that the entire band party be moved. In the end, Franksy and David manage to persuade him to stay. Quite apart from the reorganisation moving would involve, there is no other hotel in Dusseldorf at this level that can take the entire band party tonight. But Rob's not happy. He has a sore throat, too, says Josie. At the venue, he keeps to his dressing room and wardrobe mistress Flo makes him her special restorative thyme tea with honey.

Load-out Sandwich

Halfway back across the vast arena floor is the barricaded-off area where the front-of-house team mixes and monitors light and sound for the audience. On a raised dais at the back, her curly dark hair reaching almost down to her desk full of monitors and dials and computer screens, sits skinny creative director/lighting designer Liz Berry. To her left, at another set of lighting controls, is her boyish assistant Rich Gorrod, in T-shirt and long shorts, with whom she keeps up an afternoon-long flirtatious banter.

'You might be crap,' she tells him, 'but you're not cheap.'

Below is the front-of-house sound team, responsible for the mix that the audience hears. Front-centre, before a silver desk so packed with coloured knobs and slides that you could surely fly an aeroplane with it, stands Tasmanian FOH sound engineer Dave Bracey (Gabby Chelmicka's husband), assisted by sound crew Sherif El Barbari and Bart Schoonbaert, an unlikely combo of bald, bespectacled Egyptian and blond dreadlocked Belgian. It's a different world and a different set of preoccupations out here.

'Now there's a dilemma,' says Wob, as he leans in his black silk shirt against one of the rust-coloured railings that will later keep the audience at bay. 'We've got nine busloads of English in tonight. Do we play the German tape or the English tape?' They decide to play the German tape, which substitutes 'Achtung! Achtung!' for 'This is a public announcement.'

The gig is altogether more of a spectacle from here, marooned in the middle of the crowd, your view of the stage fringed along the bottom by the dark silhouettes of waving arms and hands. You appreciate the light show: the dazzling white flashes that start the gig; the orange spotlights that come on during 'Old Before I Die'; the crossing pink and white beams against the blue background during 'Road To Mandalay'.

Dave's surprisingly large hands hover over his desk, making continual tiny adjustments to the audience mix. It was an OK show, he says at the end. He makes a point of only saying something to Rob if he thinks his performance has been out of the ordinary.

'I probably make a comment once every 30 shows. There's nothing worse than having people working with you that say to you all the time, "That was fantastic! That was brilliant!" because you know that some nights you do a really great job and others you're not quite on it.' But Rob appreciates that honesty; if Dave says he's liked it, he knows it's good.

Tonight – Dave makes a face – he was so-so. There have been better gigs so far on this tour.

'Close your eyes so you don't feel them

They don't need to see you cry

I can't promise I will heal you

But if you want to I will try

To sing this summer serenade

The past is done we've both
been betrayed it's true

Some might say the truth will out

But I believe without a doubt in you'

As the band head back to the disgraced hotel, their beds or parties (and tonight for more than one, definitely, their dalliances with fans), the crew are left with the set: every last piece of which has to be dismantled, packed into the five huge Stage Trucks, and driven overnight to tomorrow night's gig in Stuttgart. They call this frenzied process, with the understatement of those who have to really sweat for their living, the 'load-out'.

With time at a premium, everything happens at once. The tall rigger in the T-shirt reading 'NORTHERN SCUM' is climbing up one of the horribly narrow ladders to unclip the chains in the roof; the lampeys are unplugging and coiling flex at the side of the stage; up on the back of the set the carpenters are tearing apart Rob's cage.

'Welcome to the mayhem,' says Little Jez, as he lowers one of Guy's guitars, a Gibson acoustic, lovingly into its deep-pink plush lined case.

Wob and his 26 members of crew now have a team of underlings to boss around: the 'local crew', whose skill and/or helpfulness varies from city to city. Dusseldorf is neither famously good nor bad, though if you were looking to cast a film about nose-ringed, long-haired, shaven-headed, multi-tattooed eco-warriors, this wouldn't be a bad place to start.

Dismantling her front-of-house lighting area, Liz Berry seems unfazed by the scary-looking help. 'You can have the heavy end cos I'm the girl,' she says to a ponytailed Visigoth who looks as if he could crush her with a single twist of his thumb.

'Excuse me, sir,' Dave says to a dawdling, lanky youth with seven rings through his nose, 'if you've got nothing to do, take this, coil it up and then put it in the box.'

There are boxes, boxes everywhere: being packed with instruments, chains, speakers, lights, monitor boards, the works, then wheeled away past supervising stage manager Gary Currier and up the long ramp and into the cold dark night and the five huge silver stage trucks that are waiting in the rain outside. 'Two more guys 'ere,' yells Gary. 'If you can help with this truck.'

You can barely hear him, for all the ear-rending clanking and crashing and banging and hammering and grinding of chains through motors that echoes around the huge arena. In the centre of the stage, a man with his shirt off, revealing an enormous black circle of a tattoo on his chest, moves down a lowered truss, straightening the individual lights.

'You burn up as many calories as any orgasm,' he grunts.

'So how many calories is that, Mr B?' asks Liz.

The 'backline crew' – drum tech Mick, guitar techs Jez and Adam, keyboard tech Jules Bowen, monitor engineer Martin and babysitter Dribble – are first to finish, peeling off cheerfully to the showers and their bus, while the lampeys and carpenters and riggers labour on. They call themselves

the Country Club, says Jez, since they leave earliest, and rise latest. The rest of the load-out is 'more of the same', he explains with a grin, till the venue is empty and the five trucks are full.

Have a shower in the morning, if you want, says Wob, leaning back from his laptop in the production office. Getting on the bus without showering is a perfectly legitimate crew alternative – Stink and Run. The load-in begins at 7.00 a.m. sharp.

There's no dinky post-gig supper on the crew buses. Instead, a hunk of French bread stuffed with ham or cheese salad, the famous 'load-out sandwich', washed down with beer or wine.

Jules is chilling downstairs, glugging Rioja from a plastic cup. It's the second night of 'three in a row' so they'll not be partying wildly tonight. She's wearing the same outfit she's worn since rehearsals in the London Arena – black T-shirt and black shorts. She only ever carries one small bag of luggage, she says, which contains her travelling wardrobe of a week's worth of black T-shirts and shorts, 'with a couple of T-shirts that aren't black for the days off'.

Upstairs, Canadian Martin has some useful tips for how to behave with the crew, first and foremost: don't shit on the bus. 'That's rule number one.' Then there's the five-minute rule: when you get up out of your seat in the lounge, you've got five minutes to reclaim your spot before someone else can take it. Finally, never wear your laminate on your day off:

that's naff and punishable with a fine of a bottle of wine.

Martin's been working for Rob since May 1999, when he was called in to do monitors on a Canadian gig and then asked to stay on. 'I don't really know much about him as a person except for what I read in the tabloids. If I get a chance to see him I'll say hello and he'll say hello, but that's pretty much the extent of our relationship. He's my boss, right. I don't think most people really hang around and spend lots of time around their boss. It's no different in this business.'

Eventually the engine starts, the gears change, and the convoy of crew buses and stage trucks moves out on to the darkness of the autobahn. Next stop, Stuttgart, and an incident that will make newspaper headlines around the world.

7

'When "Fat Bottomed Girls" comes on, at one point in the tour you've got that feeling of euphoria. You are just about to go on stage, the guitar's getting into your soul and the vocals are really pumping you up.

Then you get other days when you think, Oh "Fat Bottomed Girls" again. I've got to go on stage for the next hour and forty minutes. How the hell am I going to do that?"'

NEW ROB

7.00 a.m. The load-in begins with a series of yellow chalk crosses on the floor, scrawled out by 'Big' Jez Craddick, the lanky chief rigger who came to the business after a career in the Royal Engineers, driving and commanding land tanks. 'A friend of mine once said I was institutionalised,' he says. 'People who work in rock and roll are kind of institutionalised.'

Jez is marking out the 'points', in accordance with which Robbie's whole set – lighting and video trusses, riser, drapes, cyclorama, kabuki – will be suspended, on stage chains. 'It's entirely up to him,' says Wob, who is watching from the floor, 'to keep things absolutely accurate. He can make or break our day. If he makes a slight mistake, then nothing lands on stage.'

Meanwhile, shaven-headed ground rigger Andy Jupp and stage manager Gary Currier are getting a new local crew to unload boxes of chain and wire from the first of the five huge stage trucks outside. Besides Andy, Big Jez has two local 'up riggers' high in the roof and two 'ground riggers' on the floor. Starting from the back of the stage, they are now hanging the lighting points, chucking down wobbling lengths of blue rope. In the background, the boxes continue to roll down the ramp from the lorries.

8.30. Backstage, the five-strong catering team have unloaded their kitchen, laid their flowery plastic tablecloths out on the tables and unpacked the all-important Lavazza coffee machine. Chefs Graham Morrison and Chris Clarke are standing over sizzling pans of bacon and eggs. It's the full sit-down for the truck and bus drivers and those who aren't currently working; Mairaed DeBarra takes bacon butties out front for the riggers and lighting crew who have no free time.

9.00. With the second 'box' truck now unloaded, Gary and the local crew get to work unloading the third truck – trusses and dimmers. Back on stage, the back truss is being assembled, clanged together with half-inch steel pins from transportable sections by carpenter George Osborne, recognisable by the black hat he wears at all times. Once it's assembled and the white cyc and drapes have been hung from it, Andy attaches the bottoms of the chains.

9.30. The sound crew has appeared on the scene. Sherif and Bart are in discussion with the promoter's rep to find out just how full the arena will be tonight. When Sherif's worked out exactly where the audience will be, he gets to work with a laser, making rapid measurements of heights and distances and entering these into the software programme on his computer. Only then will he decide the final angle of the five PAs, to make sure all the audience will be covered perfectly. All his sound sources have to be 'time-aligned', so that the music right across the venue is exactly in sync.

10.00. Creative director Liz Berry has now appeared mid-arena, yawning over a coffee. From grey padded cases she unpacks her lighting desk. Out the back, the fourth truck – sound and video – is being unloaded. Up on stage, the middle lighting truss goes up, trailing six long tape measures. 'If it's not level,' Andy explains, 'the winches on the riser below will be picking up different weights. We've got a band on it, so it's very important.' Below, George gets to work assembling the riser. 'It's all just like giant Meccano, really,' he says. 'The toys just get bigger.'

11.45. The front lighting rig is now the only one left down. The rest of the stage set is wheeled across: aluminium sections with steel ends, a custom-built hook and jaw arrangement, which clips rapidly together, Rob's silver steps stage left and the slide he's never yet used stage right. Rob's famous chair is unpacked; it looks rather tame in the daylight, its luminous tendrils unlit.

12.15. The Country Club has finally put in an appearance. 'Bit of toast,' says drum tech Mick. 'Cup of tea, like, take it casual, might start a bit of work.' He, Adam, Jules and Little Jez set up their drums, keyboards and guitars on the riser. Jules tightens a blue ratchet strap. 'If all goes wrong,' she jokes, 'and the band falls off, at least the keyboard stays in place.'

She can only talk like this when the band aren't around, for in rehearsals once, the riser did go wrong, the back tilting up six inches due to 'a human error' of Big Jez's. Guy, who hates heights, had to see a hypnotist in order to be able to do the nightly descent, so there can be no mistakes again.

By 12.55, the instruments are in place and the carpenters are ready to test the mechanics. 'All right, guys, stand by!' shouts Big Jez. Up it goes, on the six alarmingly thin steel wires suspended from the truss above. A cheery Jules rides with it. The third section of black floor covering – the marley – is unrolled, and laid beneath. When it's taped down you can read Robbie's fake crest, which is painted in white. 'NON ILLEGITIMI CARBORUNDUM' – Don't Let the Bastards Grind You Down. Then 'ELVIS GRANT ME SERENITY – ROBBIE WILLIAMS A.D. 2000'.

After lunch some of the riggers and carpenters may lie down for an hour or so, on their bunks in their buses. But the load in isn't over yet. Now the stage is up and the arena can be darkened, Liz gets to work on focusing her lights. Ninety per cent of the effects, she explains, are pre-programmed. But it all gets a bit clockwork if you do everything from the programme, so she keeps a bunch of toys on her compilers so she can rush around doing manual stuff. 'I like to feel part of the show,' she explains. 'I like to use the blinders from time to time.' These are the dazzling white lights that shine out into the crowd, flashed nightly at the start. 'They're amazing things. I never knew it was a reflex action that people would scream when you poured light into their eyes, but it seems to be the way.'

The focusing is a long and laborious process, as Liz works through all the lights on each truss, checking that they're correctly aligned for the bits of stage they have to light. Eventually it's four o'clock and technical soundcheck time again. Dribble is testing the mikes. 'Gary's vocal: one two hey yeah.' Jules bangs out 'Isn't She Lovely' on Guy's keyboard. (It's one third of her famous three-song repertoire: the other two are 'Close To You' and 'Son Of My Father' by Chicory Tip.) Dave's hands hover over his desk as he gets things to his satisfaction. Work finished for the time being, Liz circles the back of the arena in her rollerblades.

When doors open at 6.30, there's a mad rush of fans to be at the front. The girls shriek as they stampede up the steps from the side corridor. Soon they are ten rows deep, chattering like starlings. They carry knapsacks and bags, so they can peel off their outer wind-jackets and coats, revealing their altogether skimpier evening outfits underneath.

When the band arrive, Tom the accountant is purring: he got lucky last night. 'And she was really cute, blonde, great body, so I'm happy.' There were four originally and he managed to whittle them down to two, in his room, drinking from the minibar. It's about time. He's been spending so much on bar bills he was starting to wonder what was happening to his ratio.

Rob walks into the male dressing room and seeing the team gathered asks everyone to 'pray silence' for a record. It's called 'Eternity', and it's their single for the summer. Everyone sits quietly, listening, as Rob nods along:

> Close your eyes so you don't feel them
> They don't need to see you cry
> I can't promise I will heal you
> But if you want to I will try
> To sing this summer serenade
> The past is done we've been betrayed it's true
> Some might say the truth will out
> But I believe without a doubt in you
>
> You were there for summer dreaming
> And you gave me what I need
> And I hope you find your freedom
> For eternity
>
> Yesterday when we were walking
> You talked about your ma and dad
> What they did that made you happy
> What they did that made you sad
> We sat and watched the sun go down
> Then picked a star before we lost the moon

Youth is wasted on the young
Before you know it's come and gone too soon

You were there for summer dreaming
And you gave me what I need
And I hope you find your freedom
For eternity

You were there for summer dreaming
And you are a friend indeed
And I hope you find your freedom
Eventually

You were there for summer dreaming
And you gave me what I need
And I know you'll find your freedom
Eventually

For eternity

'Very nice,' says Fil at the end.

'Thanks,' Rob says. He tilts his head again and wanders off, restless and fleeting as ever. He's actually a bit bored. This is mid-tour, another German town, another excited local audience, the same old jokes, the same old songs. It's not as if he's expecting anything special, as he might in Copenhagen or Paris. This is just a bog-standard gig, through which he has to strut his stuff.

Back in his dressing room he sits down with

David and launches into another game of Uno. 'Got you back!' he crows, throwing down a Reverse card. 'Classic Uno!'

The band members are equally lackadaisical, loafing around on the dressing-room sofas, bantering idly, now trying to work out exactly where in Europe they are.

'I've no idea where Stuttgart is,' says Fil.

'I've heard of it,' says Chris.

Guy comes back from the massage room. She's a bit of a cute masseuse, isn't she? For Rob. He has been known to feast on other masseuses. To pass the time, Guy suggests that everyone in the room pretend to be Dickensian and call each other by surnames only.

'What we should have is a fining system,' he says. 'If anyone doesn't use surnames. For the rest of the tour.'

'For the rest of the tour!' laughs Chris.

'Well, at least until the Brits,' says Guy.

'Mr Chambers,' says Fil, in appropriately Victorian tones, 'I put it to you that you are a complete and utter pillock.'

Pompey appears at the door, dressed in the full black regalia of the security team: black baseball cap, earphones, mouthpiece, bulging waistpack. The band want to know his second name so he can join in the game, but before anyone can start calling him Mr Wilkinson, he's off, Jonah's voice crackling out from his walkie-talkie. 'Upstage left…'

'Someone
pushed me
off stage.
It's OK.
All right.
OK, cool.'

'The last toilet before the stage is on the right at the end of the corridor,' is Pompey's parting shot. Fil raises his eyebrows and laughs. The security trio, with their elaborate, military-style procedures, are regarded as a bit OTT. On the last tour, Franksy had Jonah's catchphrase – 'Happy with that?' – printed on a T-shirt. Which Jonah, his serviceman's sense of humour fully intact, now wears on a regular basis.

John Lennon, George Harrison, Jill Dando...

In the middle of the excited pre-show crowd, Liz Berry stands behind her control desk and communicates with her team on a private network of headphones or 'cans': assistant Rich right next to her, Kiwi video supremo Alistair MacDairmid nearer the stage, and the four spotlight operators, strapped into their bucket seats high up on the front lighting truss. Three of them are drivers of the overnight buses and trucks, doubling up. 'I keep forgetting to ask,' Liz says, as the Achtung! Achtung! announcements whip the crowd up into screaming frenzy, 'what is it Rob says every night on stage in German? Presumably it's something like, "Your mother blows goats."'

'The Eagle has landed!' she cries, as Rob bounces up in his chair. Then, as he takes a new route along the top of the set away from the silver steps: 'He's come down the slide.'

'Down the slide,' echoes Rich beside her.

'Wee-hey!' she laughs. 'On your back, Robbie. OK, all stand ready for frame one. Standing by to bumper frame one, please, frame one. R-rr-ready, and go!' she orders, starting to boogy as the music begins. 'Nice,' she approves, when lighting changes go well. 'He's in a good mood tonight,' she observes. 'But not very talkative.'

After 'Forever Texas', there's another sudden surprise change in the set. Rob has decided, on a whim, to sing Noel and Liam Gallagher's hit 'Wonderwall'. He told Liz and Dave Bracey just before the show. 'I wonder if he's told the band,' Liz muses to her team. 'The entertaining thing is Yolanda's never played it before, because she didn't do the tour last year.'

As it turns out, Rob hasn't told the band. 'Fil's shitting himself,' laughs Liz. 'We're not the only ones who don't know what we're doing.' Yolanda and Fil try gamely to play the tune, but it's hardly the punchily brilliant renderings of the other well-rehearsed numbers. Then Rob forgets the words. 'What a complete disaster!' comes Alistair's Kiwi voice over the cans.

'Dat is good, ya?' goes Rob at the end, to his still enthusiastic audience.

'No,' says Alistair, 'dat is shite.'

But worse is to follow.

Halfway through the next song, 'Supreme', a tiny figure dodges round the back black curtain and races across the stage towards the star. The band and audience hardly see him, he's running so fast. For a moment, Fil thinks it's Mick, dashing on to make some adjustment on the drum dais; then, horrified, he realises it's not. For the stranger, reaching Rob, plants both palms firmly on the back of his damp black shirt and pushes him forward, right off the front of the stage.

Rob's still holding his radio mike as he falls, tumbling over the shaved head of a shocked security guard as he crashes the five feet down into the black pit below, his assailant on top of him. Diana Scrimgeour, a London rock photographer who has been shooting close-ups of Rob, drops her camera as she leaps to one side. She sees Rob's silhouetted arm as he comes over, the twisted, manic, 'really screwed-up' look on the stranger's face behind.

'He's just been attacked!' shouts Liz over the cans. There's a delayed gasp from the huge crowd, as waving hands fall rapidly to shocked sides. As the music stops, a mass chatter fills the arena. What now? Is that it? Up on stage the band members confer earnestly with each other.

For a few seconds Rob is no more than a black, sprawled heap on the floor. The security guards have dragged up the attacker and got his hands behind his back. Rob is already stirring, pulling himself into a crouch, now calling for his radio mike. David Enthoven has already jumped down and picked it up. Rob's acting almost on autopilot, but he's not going to be deterred, he's not going to call the show off – as he might have done before. He's going to get back there and finish his set. Helped by Jonah and a local security guard, Rob remounts the stage. David passes him the mike; Rob's bursting with adrenalin, he realises. Guy has now started the music, but Rob stops him with a brusque 'cut' gesture. He turns back to the crowd.

'Is everybody OK?' Rob shouts to the waiting crowd. 'Yeah,' they reassure him. 'Well, so am I,' he yells back. 'And I'm not going to let any fucker get on stage and stop you having a good time.'

There is huge applause.

'He's very shaken,' observes Alistair over the cans. 'I can tell from here. Body language. To bits.'

'I think Rob might be off for a little while, actu-ally,' says Liz, at the first break, after 'Kids'. 'Either that or race back on, bollock through it and cut straight to "Rock DJ".'

Which is what he does. He storms through his remaining numbers without a second break, ending with a "Rock DJ" that's the most energised there's yet been, an adrenalin-fuelled stormer. Then he's off and down the cloth tunnel into backstage, before anyone can say anything to him. Everyone troops after him, documentary camera crew and all. 'OK, I want everyone in here, please,' he says. He's fine, he tells them, as they crowd into his dressing room. They're not to worry. He's not going to milk the pity vibe. 'Someone pushed me off stage. It's OK. All right. OK, cool.' Everyone claps.

One Down, One to Go

Rob's dressing-room door is now closed. Manager David stands guard outside it, with the shaken-looking security guards a few yards down the corridor in a cluster. Now wardrobe mistress Flo goes in alone to minister to him. She rubs arnica tincture on his knee, gives him arnica pellets for the shock and offers something surely rarer in this ever-public circus: the love and support of a trusted employee in private. David and Josie are allowed in and Rob's brave front collapses. 'I got back on stage and I finished the gig,' he tells them. 'I couldn't ruin the show for everybody else that was out there. Because, in the past, I've had stuff thrown at me, like bottles that have hit me in the air and stuff like that and I've just walked off stage and I've not come back on. And I didn't that time, I stayed on till the end.' His voice cracks as he looks up. 'I don't know, man. It just throws loads of things like, is this worth it? You know, cos that guy stuck that knife in Monica Seles's back. He could have had a knife then. Could have had anything. I don't want to mope into the self-pity of it all or…' His voice suddenly breaks. 'But I'm scared. I'm genuinely scared,' he repeats, his eyes now glistening with tears. 'And it's not just tonight I'm scared, d'you know what I mean, it's a huge percentage of my days I'm really, really scared.'

John Lennon, George Harrison, Jill Dando, Brad Pitt. The fear that has haunted him, night after night, alone in his bedroom in Kensington Park Road, has finally become reality. Thank God it wasn't worse.

Next door, everyone is hyped and shocked and excited.

'I couldn't ruin the show
for everybody else that
was out there.
Because in the past, I've
had stuff thrown at me,
like bottles that have hit
me in the air and stuff like
that and I've just walked
off stage and I've not
come back on.
And I didn't that time, I
stayed on till the end.'

'It was like slow motion,' Fil is saying. 'I thought, Christ, Mick's moving quick…'

'He came from the back, behind the stage,' says Guy.

'How the hell, with security up the wazzoo,' says Fil, more angry than coherent, 'and he gets on stage…'

'And on top of it all,' laughs backing singer Katie, 'I lost my rose!'

Guy, who carries a little camcorder with him a lot of the time, leaving it running both on stage and backstage, has managed to catch, incredibly, the actual moment of the attack on video. They all crane over the little screen to see the assailant racing across from left to right, truly a man possessed. 'I've never seen anyone attacked on stage,' says Guy. 'And I've been to hundreds of gigs.'

Franksy arrives. The police have got the man, he tells them. He's a complete nutter, apparently. Thinks Rob is impersonating Robbie and the real Robbie Williams is somewhere else. Guy plays back the tape.

'Fuckin' 'ell!' goes Franksy.

'It's just horrible, innit?' says Guy. 'So horrible I can't bear to watch it. I've seen it about ten times,' he adds illogically.

When Rob has finally collected himself, he emerges into the corridor. Security guards Marv and Pompey are now in tears. 'Please, guys,' Rob asks the documentary camera and sound men, who have started filming and recording again. He waves them away and they back off as he goes to throw his arms around Pompey. The Falklands veteran and the superstar hug like brothers.

Ten minutes later Rob appears through the shower area that links his and the male dressing rooms at the back. He's fully dressed in black woolly hat and puffa jacket. The general chatter hushes. Spliffs go down behind armchair arms and wine glasses slide to the floor. Rob nods and smiles silently as he looks round at his band, those close to him, those he loves, he realises now more than ever, his friends. 'Are you lot going to Paris tonight?' he asks. They are. He nods again, thoughtfully. 'I might come with you,' he says. 'I'm not sure I want to stay in Stuttgart tonight.'

No, they tell him. They love him too. Come with us on the bus. Get out of Stuttgart. Leave the bloody place behind. He nods again and heads off thought-fully into the corridor.

'I couldn't believe his reaction about getting back up and finishing the show,' says David later. 'Old Robbie would have been furious and run away. This new Rob actually became this caring man that was much more concerned about everybody else not being upset. It was a turning point. The boy became a man. I was gobsmacked with pride, actually. I was in tears. I thought, "here he is, he's become a man."'

As they finish their load-out duties, the technicians

appear one by one in the hospitality room, discussing the incident as they help themselves to the band's leftover booze and wine. Little Jez can't remember the last time a fan even got on stage. Nobody particularly blames security. 'The bottom line is we all cock up on our jobs,' says Liz.

They agree that, paradoxically, it was the best 'Rock DJ' yet. 'He was high as a kite by that point,' says Liz. 'Adrenalin city.'

The load-out is finished. In the upper lounge of the production bus, the caterers are winding down big-time. It's the end of a run of three shows, tomorrow's a day off, nobody has to get up at seven and work till midnight, there's cans and bottles on the table, the music has the mellowest beat, and the air is thick with resinous fumes and laughter. One crew member says his neck feels like it's melting, he's smoked so much. As the bus rolls off down the road towards Paris, the post mortem continues.

'He only pushed him off the stage, at the end of the day,' says someone.

'Only!' cries caterer Em.

'No, I'm sorry,' says Wob crossly, standing by the open door to the stairs. 'If he hadn't landed on some security guy, that could have been Rob out for the rest of the tour, that could have been Rob's career. You know, all it takes is shaking him... If he'd pushed him any harder he'd have hit the barrier and you'd have taken his bloody jaw out... I've got friends, well, I haven't got friends, but I know people that have died falling off the stage, you know. Five foot is a long way...'

The first leg of the tour is almost over. One more gig to go and that's it, back home for the Brits and a break. There's a feeling of tired relief among the crew, as they arrive at noon through the jostling, hooting Parisian traffic and decamp with their bags at the Holiday Inn in Place de la Republique.

There's no Franksy here, with his neat white envelopes and keys to rooms that are ready. Instead, everyone camps wearily around the three armchairs by the boutique, as Wob slowly works down his list at reception. The elegant guests, pacing past in suits and ties and shimmery dresses, flick their eyes rapidly away from the unkempt platoon crowding their lobby: Bart with his magnificent blond dreadlocks; Jules in her black shorts and grubby trainers; George in his trademark black hat and the free slippers from the Atlantic Kempinsky. They're all set for their day off. Bart's talking about croissants and coffee at a place he knows round the corner. Stage manager Gary makes the gestures as he jokes about a triangular trip taking in a restaurant in Bastille, a brothel in Rue St Denis, and the cathedral of Notre Dame in Montmartre. Scoff, shag, then confess.

8 RW

'I bounced back.
I'm like a Weeble.'

ROCK DJ

Rob's fine, says David Enthoven. Happy, sad, shaken, shocked. But in a funny kind of way it was a good thing that happened last night. 'It's a wake-up call. If you do things the same way night after night, complacency is bound to set in. Thank God nothing serious happened and all he walked away with was a bruising and a real shake-up. It could have been so much worse. The lesson we have to learn from it is that he is a major icon now and we have to have every avenue blocked.'

In the plush little lobby of Hotel Le Parc, where the band is staying, Franksy, Yolanda, Tom and the blonde Paris EMI rep lounge on the orange armchairs. Guy joins the party, looking as if he's been asleep in his clothes all afternoon. They sip the complimentary champagne dispensed by the waitress and catch up on the gossip.

Rob didn't go on the coach with the band in the end, because, Yolanda leans forward and whispers with a grin, 'He feasted.' 'All night long, apparently,' adds Tom. 'She was waiting in the foyer with the thigh-high boots, then up her long luscious legs she was wearing the short black skirt. Nice arse. Black jumper. Very dark hair. Actually, quite sweet, too, so he had a good time.' Tom chuckles urbanely and glugs his champagne. 'The good thing is I'm able to live vicariously through Rob.'

While Rob and David go off to one of their self-help meetings, the remaining guys head next door to 'Alain Cass's new place' to sit up on straight-backed, white leather high chairs around a long glass table. The restaurant specialises in homard and l'agneau, which is not great for Joe Washbourn, the curly blond lead singer of Toploader (the opening act for the tour), who's a vegetarian. While he and Fil have a long insiders' chat about the industry, Guy gets stuck into ordering the wine: a Riesling Schlossberg 1996; a Chablis Domaine Defaix 1995; a Gevrey Chambertin Guyon 1990; a Nuits St George Champy 1993. Nothing but the best for the Lord.

Franksy and Josie's mobiles ring constantly. Between mouthfuls of pink lamb, Jose is sorting out Rob's appearance at the Brits on Monday and getting initial plans in place for the summer stadium tour. On the table she has a list of things to do. It reads:

1. STRING QUARTET
2. DANCERS
3. DRAGON
4. 6 x BRASS

As the group moves on to cheese, Rob appears through the swing doors of the restaurant in his big black puffa jacket. He immediately and inexorably becomes the focus as he goes round the table, chatting to the Parisian promoter, bantering with Franksy, picking up Josie's list, scrutinising it briefly and putting it down. For all his vaunted lack of confidence, he's one of those people you just can't keep your eyes off, whose powerful presence makes his mood matter to others. Now his smile curls up at the ends and everyone is happy he's happy again, back in there after his ordeal. The crisply suited management and neat waitresses hang back respectfully, with can't-quite-believe-this-celebrity-is-here smiles on their faces. Rob's eyes swoop down over the glasses of red and white wine and suddenly he's off, mercurial as ever. Josie puts down her cheese, picks up her mobile and hurries after him.

I Want Sainsbury's
The Paris Zenith is the grooviest venue yet, a huge aluminium tent of an arena. Inside, everything's magnificently French. The banks of red seats are filled with people laughing and talking in an immensely civilised way, as if this were a concert, not a gig. Jazzy violin music plays. You almost expect to see Serge Gainsbourg strolling down the steps with a Gitane between his lips.

There's a new security man, Max, shaven-headed, black and silent, to add to the existing trio, whose alertness is now evident in their every nervy move.

Backstage is tiny: all the dressing rooms are

Portakabin-type structures opening on to the central catering area. It's like the set for some cheesy musical about rock 'n' roll. Rob's dressing room is up a narrow spiral staircase, and he's sitting back on the couch in his white dressing gown, talking about how he's feeling after being pushed off stage.

'Everything is really cool. It's going splendiferous. I feel really loved by everybody: the crew, by everybody that's around me, security.' The other night was terrifying though. 'One minute I'm on stage in the middle of a show that I was really bored doing, then the next I'm in the pit and there's this man jumping on top of me wanting to batter me. My first thought was, old me would have used that as an excuse to cancel the tour, but I'm feeling much healthier these days. I just wanted to go back on and finish the show. It gave me the impetus and the adrenalin to get back up and perform the best I'd ever performed in the last few numbers.

'But I will say this touring lark isn't for me. Not any more. I can't stand the rollercoaster of emotion. The one crowd that's good and the one crowd that's bad. Me singing the songs that I'm bored of and haven't got great feeling for any more. I've lost perspective on what the songs are about or how they made me feel at the time of writing them. Right now they're all just a pile of shite. It's difficult to do every night, but I'm looking forward to tonight and I'm looking forward to going home tomorrow.'

But that toxic head of his is better. He shrugs and

smiles. 'But there's always an ism here or there. An ism of self doubt or an ism of…but yes, it's getting a lot better, thank you very much.'

So he's bounced back?

'Yeah, I bounced back. I'm like a Weeble.'

The Saturday night crowd is rocking. Liz's blinders flash in their eyes. 'Robbie! Robbie!' rings out over the din. The huge kabuki curtain falls.

Then disaster strikes.

At the very top of its lift, the riser gets stuck. It doesn't move, just wobbles, swaying very slightly from side to side. Rigger Jez and keyboard tech Jules, who are up there with the band, are not worried. They know how the system works. If the computer fails, the motor locks. There's no danger of it falling, and there's a back-up computer ready to take over.

But this is Guy's worst nightmare. Though he admits he likes the effect of the kabuki dropping to reveal the bare stage, then the band coming down from on high, the actual doing of it has been a nightly torture for him. He looks up to see the thin steel wires slowly unravelling from the lighting truss above; he knows that that truss is itself suspended each day from yet more thin steel wires in a new roof. Jez and his riggers are very, very good at their job, but he feels the terrifying precariousness of the whole thing. And there's always human error, isn't there? If somebody as obviously competent as Jez can do it once… Guy tries to stop thinking, to calm himself by staring fixedly at the notes on his keyboard. He can feel his legs trembling.

Down below, Rob can see what's happened from his chair. He's not too worried. This is great, he thinks, I'll just start the show without the band and then they'll come down. Rock'n'roll. Just me and a stage and no band. Brilliant. 'Get me up, get me up,' he says to Gary and Sarne. So they activate the counterbalance, Rob bounces up, the cheers redouble, and he runs down his stairs to the front of the stage. And suddenly… nothing. Rob remembers only then that he takes his cue for 'Let Me Entertain You' from Guy, who is stuck on the riser.

'So there was just me stood there,' he says, 'realising that I wasn't going to be able to sing. Looking at the audience and thinking, I've really ballsed up here.'

As Rob turns to walk off, Wob runs on. He's been cueing house lights from the wrong part of the building and wasn't immediately on the spot. He stands central on the stage, cursing himself for his complacency, shaking visibly in his black silk shirt. 'Ladies and gentlemen, due to a technical problem we'll have to stop the show for a minute.'

The crowd, uncertain for the last half-minute, now boo loudly. This is like Tea in the Park in Glasgow, Wob thinks, when the monitor failed and he had to take the band off stage. Then he had 30,000 booing at him.

'I'm very sorry,' he shouts to the mass of hostile faces. 'We'll get this going.'

As the lampeys and carpenters work frantically to switch to the back-up computer, Rob has retreated to the side of the stage. High above, Guy is still staring at the notes on his keyboard. He's not looking up, he's not looking down. Chris has got off his stool and is lying flat on his back to keep calm. He's checked out Jez's face: he seems cool, so, yeah, just don't think about it. Fil is also lying flat on the floor of the riser. How long have they been up here? It must be a good five minutes. The cheering, then booing, has long since died to a distant confused chattering.

And then, suddenly, absurdly, to a burst of dinner jazz that very definitely isn't 'Let Me Entertain You' the riser starts to descend. As they come into the stage light, Guy looks white. He looks up, shakes his head over at Fil and mouths, 'I'm not doing that again.'

The riser is on the floor. Fil and Yolanda and Gary step off as Rob runs out to centre-stage. 'So much for the big intro, folks,' he yells. 'Let's rock!'

And he does, giving them his all. 'I want to see those hands.' 'I want you all to go bouncy-bouncy.' 'I know I'm no-o-ot a hopeless case.' 'Merci beaucoup.' 'You've got great lungs.' 'Ecoutez! Ecoutez!'

'I got pushed off stage,' he tells them just before 'Better Man'. 'Didn't I? But I'm still here, aren't I? They knock me down and I come back stronger. Ladies and gentlemen,' he adds, just before his 'Supreme' intro, 'this is for anybody that's thinking of pushing me off stage in the future: You don't want to fuck with Robbie.'

'I'm a bad man,' he adds, and then makes a stabbing motion downwards to his invisible assailant. 'Keep down, you sucker.'

Backstage, Guy isn't happy. He's never going up on that riser again, he says. Wob appears in the dressing room to make a little speech. He just wants to tell everyone that there was no danger whatsoever at any point. Unfortunately, the computer had an error, which meant that effectively they couldn't turn on the motor to bring the riser down. It wasn't a question of anything falling. 'We just couldn't start the winches.'

The band barrack him with objections and he seems cross they're so upset. 'You didn't have to go out in front of 7,000 people booing you,' he says.

'You didn't have to sit 30 feet above the stage,' says Fil.

'Look, if you have any problems, look over at Jez. If you see him freaking out that's when you've got to worry.'

'That's reassuring,' says Guy, dryly.

'This is the third mishap we've had in a week,' says Yo.

'Words fail me,' says Fil.

'I want Sainsbury's, I want Tesco's, I want a normal life,' says Yo.

Dirty Little Slag
Back at Le Parc, the post-gig supper is at a long table

in a pretty dining room at the back, with white curtains and bowls of white flowers under a conservatory-style glass roof. David Enthoven is relieved to have got the first half of the tour finished. But he only really feels he can relax when it's all over, he says.

Rob is sitting next to a pretty, fragile-looking blonde in a white jacket; next to her is an older woman. It's not a girlfriend, nor even a fan, but a young lady from Newcastle who has leukaemia and can't find a bone-marrow match. She wrote to Rob, she says, and he met her backstage at one of his gigs. 'In Glasgow,' Rob continues. 'Joanne came backstage with her mum and a friend of hers. And we sat down and chatted. Over the last year and a half, maybe two years, I've found it increasingly difficult to talk to anyone, because my confidence went. So I was overwhelmed when Joanne came back and I had a conversation with her. And it flowed freely. We started chatting and we just really got on. She's a really special lady, absolutely beautiful, with a lovely heart. We've been exchanging phone calls ever since.'

Joanne hasn't found her bone-marrow match yet. 'But there's always a yet,' says Rob. And Rob himself is going to go on the list for the bone-marrow donor thing. 'Hopefully I can be a possible match for somebody.'

'Shall we play that game we played at Jane Seymour's house?' says Rob, when the meal is almost over. It's that old parlour game known as What's In

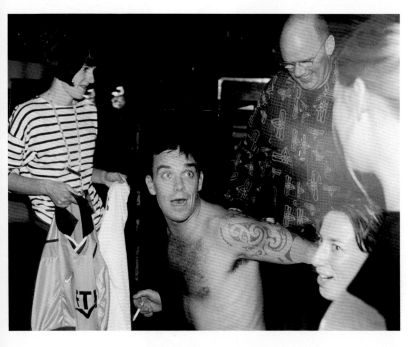

The Bag?, renamed Dirty Little Slag by Rob, where names of famous people are put in a hat and each team has to work out who they are from their representative's description. So we all start writing down ten names each, on torn slips of paper, which are put into a big silver bowl. Having suggested the game, Rob then heads off upstairs. With the prime mover gone, the enthusiasm dwindles rapidly around the long table. 'If he doesn't come down, I'm going out,' says Chris.

But Rob's soon back and taking charge of the re-energised party. An empty chair on the side of the table nearest the wall is the 'hot seat'. Two teams are chosen. One by one the participants go up and pull out names from the heap of paper in the silver bowl. Rob's very much the master of ceremonies, introducing each new person with, 'Pray silence for…'

You see people in a new light. Jonah quotes Wordsworth's 'I wandered lonely as a cloud'. The documentary crew's silent Cumbrian loader Michael Timney is revealed as a chatty wit who thinks Loyd Grossman is 'a right pain in the arse'. And when Rob gets to the hot seat himself, he's surprisingly hesitant and longwinded about describing people.

But his name keeps coming up. It's as if his entourage can't get him out of their minds, even when they're relaxing. 'Sounds like Rob without the R' is the way someone gets to Asterix's Obelix. Then there's Rob Roy and Robin Williams, not to mention Robin Hood.

'The Brits was about going there, receiving my awards, being humble – as I am – saying thank you and trying to believe that I deserve it. And then coming home and having a cup of tea and playing cards and chatting to a few close friends, discussing the evening and going to sleep.'

Most around the table have tactfully switched from wine to water now. Gabby's still on the red wine, and documentary director Brian sneaks in a quick glass. Franksy and Josie have retreated to another room, taking their (full) glasses with them.

At the end of the game, Guy stands up and says he wants to go out. Fil and Yolanda do too. There's a party for Robbie at the VIP club on the Champs Elysées. Rob's not interested. He'd much rather play another round of Dirty Little Slag. But his will is not going to rule tonight, on this last night of the leg. He's outnumbered by would-be dancers. He shrugs and goes off upstairs to the world of water, taking Joanne and her mum with him. The night after his trauma it's good to be able to relax with this unusual friend, an ordinary person he can talk to in an ordinary way, not some crazed fan, gobsmacked with adoration.

The 'other half of Robbie Williams', meanwhile, sits in the VIP section of the VIP club, getting over his earlier panic and chuckling quietly at all the waitresses dressed in blue Robbie T-shirts. It's great, he thinks, that his musical partner so rarely comes out on the town these days. It makes these sort of hideous night people want him all the more.

Oh, My Little Sausage
Robbie's going home for the Brits. In the Club Lounge of Charles de Gaulle airport, the band mem-

bers leaf through the papers. Guy's checking out the property section, still looking for his dream house in north London. 'The Uruguayan Embassy's up for sale for £17 million,' he says. 'That's a nice gaff.' He reads on. 'There's an apartment here in Mayfair – an apartment – for 3.5 million.'

'Where?' asks Franksy.

'Upper Grosvenor Street.'

'Upper Arse Street,' says Franksy.

Gabby brings over a lonely hearts mag for Tom. 'Thought this might be your kind of thing,' she says with a grin.

Rob is taking the Eurostar, to outwit the press. But when the band land at Heathrow there's not a paparazzo to be seen. They are swept to Earl's Court in a fleet of shiny black limousines. Rob has already arrived backstage, strolling up and down with David and Josie on the red carpet outside the makeshift complex of dressing rooms. He's immediately on duty, led to a couch by celebrity interviewer Kate Thornton, who fires questions at him for a webcast interview. Is he really going out with Geri? How's he enjoying the tour? What are his plans for next year? He's going to have a year off, he says, try and find himself. Where? 'I'm going to stay at home and have a good look around the house,' he jokes. 'See if I can find myself there.'

On the other side of the huge black dividing curtain, in the vast arena of Earl's Court, the front-of-stage area is full of milling people. A team of TV guys pushes a massive camera back and forth on rails. High above, a mad little moving eye of a lens zooms up and down on its own crazy track. The band is on stage, complete with a three-man brass section, half of the six who'll go with Robbie on the summer stadium tour. To the right, on big, diagonally criss-crossed screens that resemble Marshall speakers, are the sexily gyrating silhouettes of four female dancers. David and Tim chat with the chairman of EMI, Tony Wadsworth, who's also, intriguingly, the organiser of this year's Brits. Josie talks to Sergio Covino, the 28-year-old dancer who's going to impersonate Robbie for 40 seconds on Monday night. Dressed up in the skinned body gear from the 'Rock DJ' video, he's going to make a distracting entrance on a bridge over the audience while Rob himself emerges from a hole at the centre of this silver cone of a set, which looks like a giant Walnut Whip, with steps running down the front between big blow-up models of the nine Brits he has already won. It's absolutely confidential at the moment, Tim says, but he's going to win three more on Monday, putting him well into double figures, an all-time record.

At first attempt, the revolving stage fails to revolve and Wob and some of the crew have to push it. 'Does this remind anyone of anything?' says Fil loudly.

Rob wanders on stage and stands central by his mike. Above the set, his blown-up image is repeated fourfold on the giant video screens.

'My name is Robbie Williams,' he improvises into the mike. 'I come from Stoke-on-Trent. I went to school where I got bullied a bit…'

He's in an obviously good mood today, horsing around in his jeans and pale blue shirt, now pretending to be an American country music singer. 'Keep rolling, rolling, rolling,' he sings. Then he's David Bowie. Then some German-style liedermeister, singing operatically: 'Oh-h, the sun is shining… Oh-oh-over the hills come… a sausage and a little man… Oh-h, his name is sau-sage…'

Five minutes later this has become the chorus of an absurd little song. 'Oh-oh, my little sausage,' he sings. 'That's the single for the summer, Tony,' he shouts down to the chairman of EMI.

'Organised chaos,' laughs David. 'It'll all come together by Monday.'

'Oh, my little sausage,' sings Rob. 'You bring me joy, but you also bring me… dismay.' He looks dramatically over towards an imaginary horizon. 'You bring me dismay. You also bring me dis tune and dis life,' he riffs.

Now he's run up to the top of the flight of steps, climbed into the centre of the set. 'Oh, the little sausage,' he sings, 'disappearing down a ruddy great hole.'

He's gone.

'Show begins in ten seconds,' shouts Wob. 'Six, five, four…'

'Oh-h-h!' comes Rob's scream from deep inside

the hole. 'It's friggin' Liam Gallagher. He's got me by the throat.'

There's laughter all round, dying as he appears, head rising slowly above the set. ''Allo, beetches!' he cries from the top of the steps. Then he turns into profile, holds up his mike: 'Oh-h-h, my little sausage…'

He comes down and they perform 'Rock DJ', not very well. 'I'll do it proper on Monday, don't you worry,' Rob tells everyone. Then, mock-sternly: 'I expect to see you all on Monday. Bring your little sausages with you. I am going home to watch Match of the Day. And he's off, back to the flat in Kensington Park Road, with its big blue couch in front of the huge wide-screen TV, its shelves of cuddly toys, its Darth Vader figure and its signed Port Vale football.

'Everybody stay where you are!' shouts Wob. 'Don't even think of leaving.' The whole manoeuvre must be rehearsed again, though this time Wob takes the Principal's place, emerging slowly from the hole with a giant grin on his face, which is picked up and magnified on the four huge video screens above. Wob walks slowly down the steps and stands sheepishly in front of the mike in his leather jacket and blue jeans, his big shiny hair swaying slightly. As 'Rock DJ' proceeds, he grins, nervously strokes his stubble and almost, at one point, starts to dance. All is magnified fourfold above and one thing's for sure – nice guy though he is, Wob isn't Rob.

Ego A Go-Go

Two nights later the Earl's Court auditorium has been transformed into a vast and gorgeous undersea cavern. Blue and orange beams pierce the gloom, sending light dancing off the shiny gold chairs ranged round each circular table, the glittering glasses and bottles awaiting the distinguished music industry guests. Waiters and waitresses, with neat white aprons at their waists, loiter in groups, watching the action.

Down on stage, Wob and his crew are setting up for the 'Rock DJ' opener. It's not going well. At the dress rehearsal earlier, the revolve didn't work again. The band, says Fil, were not impressed.

'This doesn't feel as if it's London,' says Gary.

'Could be an awards ceremony in Germany,' says Guy.

'The Blitz!' says Chris, with his habitual punch-line-enforcing laugh.

At 5.30 Rob arrives backstage in a posse. Besides David, Josie, Jonah and Marv, there's Rob's best mate, Jonathan Wilkes, who normally accompanies Rob on tour, but has been busy in the last few weeks launching and promoting a pop career of his own. He's five years younger than Rob, and his mother was Rob's mum's best friend, so the pair were brought up like brothers in Stoke-on-Trent. Another friend with a round face and long hair is a scriptwriter from LA. The boss pokes his nose round the door of the male dressing room.

'Hi, fellas.'

His eyes flick round the room and he's gone, back into his own dressing room to change into a dark blue Indian-style shirt with elaborate silver patterning down the front.

'You need an elephant,' says Guy, who's wandered in with Kylie Minogue. He and Rob have written her a new song, 'Your Disco Needs You'.

Round the corner, past Eminem's room, marked by a trio of enormous security men, is the Scarlet Club Room and Lounge, done out like an upmarket bordello, with crimson carpets, banks of vermilion Dutch tulips, a mirror-ball throwing darts of light on the white canvas ceiling. Graham Norton hangs by the bar in a pink suit. Two very tall and elaborately dressed black ladies recline centrally on red, silver and white cushions. Katie Kissoon stands at the entrance, with a cup of tea, laughing at the scene. Neither she nor Tessa is staying for the party, needless to say. Franksy neither. 'What would I want to go for?' he says. 'The public are out there.'

'It's so frightening,' chuckles Gary, returning from a backstage tour. 'Ego a go-go.' He changes into his standard stage outfit, the blue and white checked calico shirt and the fawn cotton trousers. Fil appears. He's tense, too, as he puts on a kilt.

French Flo glides back and forth in her leather trousers, quietly sorting out wardrobe, sewing on a button here, pressing a shirt there, making honey tea for Rob who stands in his doorway, made up, looking seriously freaked out.

'I love the people of Stoke-
on-Trent, it's where I'm from,
and I'll never forget that, but
it's not where I'm at.

Every time I go back to
Stoke something has closed
down, industries, coalmines.

But Stoke people are the
most lovely people, the
funniest and most humorous.
I want to give them a lot back
because a great deal of what
they are has made me what
I am today.'

'Good luck, Rob.'

'Thank you,' he replies dazedly. 'Everything will be cool. Life is beautiful.'

Guy returns to change. 'Did you see Eminem rapping outside his room?' He laughs. 'Just rapping to people passing. Definite Brits moment.'

Suddenly it's three minutes to the show and time to do the huddle. Rob is concerned to get everyone in. 'Get Max,' he shouts. They do the Elvis prayer. Rob wishes everyone luck. Then: 'If I get through tonight without getting battered or pissed it'll be a miracle.'

White spotlight beams swerve in circles over the screaming, cheering crowd. The stage erupts in yellow flashes. 'ROBBIE,' says the huge white capitals which dominate the stage, below the stern troupe of giant Brits behind. 'Robbie! Robbie!' goes the soundtrack.

And here he is! 'Britain's biggest popstar' the *Sun* will call him tomorrow morning, when they crown him 'KING ROB' on their front page. Boogying down between the tables from right at the back in the full 'Rock DJ' skinless, bloody make-up.

'Robbie-eeeeeee! Robbie!' it climaxes. And this time, incredibly, the stage revolves and, as the band replaces the Brits, five plumes of white smoke erupt from the centre of the Walnut Whip. Audience heads swivel. Girls gasp visibly. It was all a decoy. For here is the real Robbie, rising, Christ-like, from the Wobhole, hands folded modestly before him, simply clad in white T-shirt under black suit. He steps forward, pauses for a moment to tug his left ear to the screams, grins his flat gibbon grin as he runs down the steps to hurl himself into 'Rock DJ'. 'Me with the floorshow, kicking with your torso…'

Behind their giant speaker screen, the wildly gyrating silhouetted dancers have feathers in their hair. Guy looks like a Sinister Mr Big in black suit, black shirt, black tie, dark glasses, upright as he jams with his fingers on the keyboards. Fil leaps around in his kilt. Gary taps his foot. As he finishes, Robbie punches the air and bows. The MasterCard Brits 2001 are upon us, with hosts Ant and Dec.

The IE Music party has two tables out front. One, water only, is for Rob, his best mate Jonathan, his LA chum Sacha, David, Tim, Josie and special guest Geri Halliwell, tiny in white boots, a narrow white leather skirt, and a gold butterfly bustier with no back. Just behind on a second alcoholic table, are Fil, Guy, Gabby and the rest of the IE staff who keep the show going in London. Sacha's had an idea for the cameras. 'When Rob wins his first award,' he says, 'nobody cheer.' Rob can go, 'I've won,' pretending he's really surprised, and everyone else, at both tables, 'can just shrug and look bored.'

And who should be announcing the first award – for Best British Male Solo Artist – but is-she-isn't-she girlfriend Geri 'And who would you most like to win tonight?' asks Dec, leering in contemporarily ironic fashion as he mentions Robbie among the five nominations. Geri returns the face. 'OK, let's milk it a bit,' she says, as she pauses on the opened envelope.

'I'll give you a clue. He's very male, he's very healthy, he's a talented artist, he's got the biggest heart, and, wait for it, according to the press he's been giving me one. So let me return the favour by giving him one. My very dear friend, Mr Robert Williams.'

'I've won!' goes Rob, and both tables ignore him as planned. 'So?' says Jonathan Wilkes. Rob shrugs theatrically and heads off into the limelight. Unfortunately the TV cameras miss the whole tableau.

Despite the jokes this is an incredibly tense evening for Rob. This ceremony is the scene of more than one classic Robbie outburst. 'He was all over the place,' says Jonathan. 'He doesn't like seeing other celebrities, doesn't know how to deal with them. Sometimes I even become the mouth for Rob. He'll say, "This is my mate Jonathan," and bring me in straightaway, because I'll talk. I'll prompt all the conversation. Also, with awards, he doesn't feel as if he deserves them.

'He didn't know what he was going to say on stage. Then he was worried someone was going to take a pop at him. Because normally people invade the stage.'

But tonight, New Rob has taken over. As he accepts he says, 'I normally stand up here and say something stupid, like ask to fight somebody, or, you know, make a quip or have a laugh. I always stand up 'ere, and do that, because I never thought I deserved it before and right now this is my – I don't know – fourth year of coming back and being given awards and I'm going to say nothing except, "I thank you very much."' It's a triumphant moment, in a whole new way.

In the backstage monitor area, Canadian Martin and Grubby are sharing a beer. Martin is laughing at the Destiny's Child monitor man, who's boogying along as he does the sound for his group. 'Dancing monitor engineer!' he laughs. 'You don't often see one of those these days.'

There's a roar and 'Rock DJ' is on the sound system. Rob's won his second Brit – Best British Video (for 'Rock DJ'). This time both his tables applaud, and Geri leans over to kiss him. As Rob mounts the platform, he gives Graham Norton a celebrity clinch. He thanks the crowd, then dedicates the award to his nephew, Freddie Robert, who's now five months old: 'And your mum can play this video-tape back to you, Freddie, of when your uncle was famous.'

He's taking nothing for granted, Rob, even now.

When Eminem appears, in mask, with chainsaw, Rob stands to watch, the back of his neck as clipped as Sinatra's. At the end of the song he punches his fist in the air. He loves Eminem. 'I think he's a lyrical genius, he's fucking Shakespeare – absolutely amazing.'

Robbie wins his third Brit – for Best Single

('Rock DJ'). With a soberly nervous smile on his face, he thanks everyone except his musicians. 'What about the band?' shouts Chris from the table. 'You'll have to excuse the big security presence with me,' Rob adds. 'It's not that I'm getting all big-time. It's just that someone might try and throw me off stage. I'm going home now,' he concludes. He knew all along that he'd won three.

He sweeps back to the flat with Jonathan Wilkes, Geri and Josie. While Josie goes out to get some takeaway sea bass from a local restaurant, Rob and Jonathan change out of their suits. Johnny puts his shorts on as always, while Rob slips into pyjamas. There's a game of Uno, a pot of tea and a bit of a laugh about the evening, then it's upstairs to bed. 'What d'you expect me to do?' says Rob. 'I've done those ceremonies, I've done those awards. I've been at those parties. I've done it, three times over. I've taken drugs with everybody there is to take drugs with. I've done everything that is needed to do regarding drink. There is sod all at those things apart from pissed-up people looking for celebrities. And I've met the celebrities and now I am one. One that they come and have a look at. What's the point of going out? It's not fun. You have to be pissed to enjoy it. And then all hell breaks loose. With me, anyway. No, for me, there's no point. If you've got nothing to say to anybody anyway, you might as well go home and have a cup of tea and watch telly.'

This is not a point of view, however, shared by Fil

and Gabby and the team of attractive young women who run the IE Music mission control in London. Tonight is a definite jolly for them all and they are not going to be put off by the Ali G lookalike bouncer who guards the damp and freezing flight of concrete steps at the side of Earl's Court and needs to see the right ticket for everyone, please. Eventually Gabby has sorted it and the girls are allowed to climb aboard green canvas rickshaws pedalled by cheery Antipodeans which speed them down a long underground concrete tunnel to a reception committee of yet more glowering heavies, this gang patrolling a giant goods lift. Clanking up in that, they are finally released into the U2 party. There's no sign of Bono, who Rob says he would be if he had to come back as any other living singer. Instead, a pre-party table full of tequila shots, free tubes of Berocca vitamin supplement ('for hectic lifestyles'), free morning-after pills (only kidding), then upstairs to a white muslin tent where the crowd queues at a bar for exotic cocktails and Thai food served in half-coconuts. Little white dots of light are projected everywhere: on the drapes; on the white sofa where a couple snog as if the world was ending; on Graham Norton, chatting keenly with celebrity castaway Ben Fogle; and on the longest serving of the IE girls, suddenly in tears with the emotion of it all. On each side are even more exclusive VIP areas; in one, Eminem sits alone with his heavies, looking thoroughly bored.

'KING ROB' shouts the front page of next morning's Sun. 'OUR GREATEST POP STAR WINS THREE MORE BRITS' continues the sub-headline below. 'ROBBIE'S A THREE BRIT HERO' yells the Mirror. Even the Independent manages a photograph of the black-suited, haunted-eyed star on its front page.

'Every time I go to those award ceremonies,' Rob says, the next day, as he sits back on the big blue sofa in the Notting Hill flat, 'I always end up feeling less than everybody else, in that they're cooler than me, their songs are better than mine, they're handling the whole thing better than me. I always want the ground to open up whenever I'm speaking to any of my peers, like Bono or Elton John. I just don't feel worthy enough to be in their company or their presence. If I speak to them for too long then they're going to know I'm a charlatan and I'm just not worthy of being around them. What the Brits was beautiful for this year was the fact that it was the first time I'd been to an award ceremony and I didn't feel more than anybody and, more importantly for me, I didn't feel less than anybody. I don't know about award ceremonies, I really don't. I don't know what's fixed and what isn't fixed.

'I'd like to believe that the general public voted for it because they really liked it. And if they did, I'm really, really pleased. I'm honoured that they took the time out of their day to spend 50p to phone up a line that said, "We think Robbie should win it." Because

normally on those sort of things, it's won by whoever's the biggest boy band at the time. Because the
only people that can be bothered to get off their
arses are teenagers or younger than teenagers. My
audience has changed an awful lot. A lot of teenagers
still come, but now there is more of the over-20
crowd, the over-25 crowd, the couple crowd. I just
wouldn't have expected to have won such an award,
voted by the public. So I'm very honoured, very
pleased and very happy that they have phoned up
and said, "We think you're all right Rob. We want
you to have that award because we like you. We like
your music. We like what you're about." That
touches me.

'The whole Brits thing is geared around the
people at the tables or in the audience, they've come
to have a look at a star and take a memory back with
them – and invariably it's also about getting drunk or
taking cocaine or ecstasy or whatever mood-altering
substance you can get hold of. I find the pressure of
turning up to a place that's full of your peers and
feeling like you don't deserve it and having that
much attention thrown at you while you're in a
shame spiral about not deserving what you're getting
– I normally get rat-arsed because of it.

'This year it wasn't about that for me. It couldn't
be about that for me. The Brits was about going
there, receiving my awards, being humble – as I am –
and saying thank you, and trying to believe that I
deserve it. And then coming home and having a cup

of tea and playing cards and discussing the evening and going to sleep. It wasn't get pissed at the table because you can't handle it; get up to receive an award that you don't think you should have and swear an awful lot and make a joke out of the whole thing and be thoroughly disgusted with the whole event for it being manufactured and industry-orientated or, you know, offer somebody on in a fight. I really tried to go up there and say thank you and believe I deserved it. And there was twenty per cent of me this time that believed I did. The rest didn't. And there was also a quarter of me that thought, "I should have won four." So there is a huge ego mixed with the same huge insecurity and lack of self-worth on the other side, that goes, "I don't deserve this, but I should have won another award." '

And this is a man who is on the front of every newspaper. The country – or at least the media – love him today. Surely that should calm his insecurities? Rob shakes his head.

'All that just frightens me. I don't have tabloid newspapers in my house. Because it distorts my image of me. It distorts what I believe myself to be. Because they've got this person they are claiming I am and more often than not the person that they claim I am is conceited and needs to be brought down a peg or two. And if I read that I believe that I'm shit. I believe that I'm a megalomaniac, arrogant, a sex maniac, whatever they want to write. So I don't read it any more and it's doing me the world of good. But somebody had the paper in their house when I went round and it was like an addiction. I couldn't help looking at it. I only saw the front page and I saw the title "King Rob" and that was enough for me. I took it out of his hands and threw it in the bin.

'You know... I write some records with the help of Guy. I sing them and I perform them. I might bring a lot of joy and a lot of love into people's lives. I might touch them and if I do then that's wonderful, but I'm not saving lives. I'm not doing heart operations or finding bone marrow for people. They're the real heroes. I'm just a very lucky... I've worked really damn hard... I'm a 27-year-old that comes from Stoke-on-Trent... Very average when I was a kid... Very, very average and I'm very average now. I just have an extraordinary life. And to have something bestowed on me as King Rob or anything like that, a quarter of my ego quite likes it and the rest of me just pales away and goes, "I don't want that. That's scary."'

9

'Every Sunday I would go into the front room and put on records. It would always be Nat King Cole, Sammy Davis Jnr, Dean Martin, Frank Sinatra, Sarah Vaughan and Ella Fitzgerald.

I would learn the words and memorise the songs and disappear into that era. I think the first CD I ever bought was Glenn Miller.'

CAN YOU KICK IT?

It's been a bit of a strange tour so far, Guy thinks. What with Rob being pushed off stage, the riser getting stuck, the revolve not working at the Brits. But it's really great to be so popular in Europe. 'There's nothing more exciting than a sell-out tour, when people really, really want a ticket, a hot, hot ticket.'

Rob's keeping clean and starting to enjoy himself has been the other remarkable novelty of the first half. Gary's been on tours with him before where he hasn't. 'You can tell he's not enjoying it, so everyone is a bit edgy. Whereas if the centre person is happy, then it makes everyone else kind of happy, which is how it should be. Funnily enough, I asked him just before Stuttgart, "Are you enjoying it?" And he said, "Yeah, more than ever." And that night,' Gary chuckles dryly, 'he was pushed off the stage.'

David is still very proud of the way Rob managed Stuttgart. 'He would have been perfectly justified in buggering off back to England after that. I suppose for me it's been a bit like seeing my favourite son have a spiritual awakening.'

But is Rob going to manage to keep it up? Franksy's pretty impressed with Rob's forbearance so far. In the old days, as he's said, Rob would sooner or later relapse. Then the beers led to the drugs. 'And the music business goes hand in hand with drugs. Trying to keep them away from people is hard. Rob freely admits that he had a lot of friends in a lot of circles. You go back to a city, somebody remembers the last time you used to do some drugs, so they turn up and straight away they put it in your hand. You want it, but you don't want it, and it's like, What am I going to do now? So it's a constant pressure. I think that's the hard part and why there's this cocoon round him as well. We're just constantly on vigil to make sure that somebody doesn't slip through and upset all the hard work that's been done by David and Tim in helping Rob get on the straight and narrow.'

Assuming the best, everyone returns to Germany. The crew rendezvous on Thursday evening in King's Cross, where some over-indulge in the Offshore Bar before falling on to their tour coaches at 11.30 for the eighteen-hour drive to Nuremberg. Star and band fly out the following evening, arriving at the Meridian Hotel just as the crew members are having a final drink before bed.

Rob arrives first. Against the black-streaked, orange marble of the lobby, he waits with his entourage for the lift. Then he turns, sees a gang of crew in the bar, and comes through. 'How are you all? All's right in the world,' he says, eyes swivelling round.

'That's why I like working for him,' enthuses Em, when he's gone, as quickly as he appeared. 'He saw us, at the stairs, and came over. He really didn't have to do that.' He's still human, she elaborates. 'He hasn't become... just rock.'

Then she's laughing about Stuttgart. 'Thank God it doesn't happen to caterers,' she says. 'I mean, it's not like anyone's going to come into the kitchen and say, "You're not the real Em, are you?"'

Big Jez the rigger appears, back from dinner with Wob's production assistant Lizzie. 'That's a relatively recently declared tour relationship,' Em observes. The pair have a quick drink and retire upstairs, to do 'office work'.

'Enjoy your filing,' shouts Em, after them.

Then the band is here. Guy in heavily patterned trousers and a blue coat. Yolanda and Claire. Fil. Joe from Toploader.

The circus is back on the road.

What No Kabuki?
At around ten o'clock the next morning there's a crisis. The new black front curtain – the kabuki – which was ordered over the break, because the old one was dying a death, hasn't got all its correct parts: there are five cables and 30 hangers missing. Andy Jupp runs out to production to consult Wob, and Wob is immediately on the phone to the suppliers in the UK. 'We've got a guy going out to the airport now,' he says, 'to bring out the right bits. Otherwise

we haven't got a show.'

'You can't do the show without it?'

Wob purses his lips. 'No.'

'What a sodding disaster,' says Andy. 'I'd have stayed in bed on Monday if I thought this was going to happen.'

So the front truss stays down for the time being, while everything else is put in place ready. The lights, the riser, the backstage, the video equipment.

At four o'clock the parts still haven't arrived. Dave Bracey presses on with his soundcheck. 'OK, Julesy, please.' She sits at Guy's keyboard and plays 'Isn't She Lovely'.

At six, at last, there's good news. The kabuki bits are in Frankfurt... but won't be here till seven at the earliest.

Backstage, Wob's got another headache.

'Go through what happened in Paris,' says Guy.

Wob repeats his explanation of why the riser didn't work. The old computer had an error, which meant the winches couldn't be started. Now they've got a new computer.

'Even better,' chips in Franksy, with his heaviest Bristolian irony, 'things are even better.'

'What are the chances of it happening again?' asks Guy.

'The same as your grandfather being struck by lightning,' teases Chris.

Wob remains serious, arguing his point. Even if

the new computer crashed, which won't happen, the platform can't fall. 'The riser motors are of a type that they are locked into whichever position they are in, until they're told to do otherwise. If all six motors don't do exactly the same thing, then they stop automatically…'

The boss has appeared, immediately taking attention from Wob's elaborate explanation.

Rob has flu and is a little mournful today. He sits down and picks up his guitar. 'This is the end,' he sings, as Wob departs, back to the real world.

> I'm in pieces, I don't know what to say.
> Do you think it's best if I told her that I was gay?
> I'm not really, but the truth is too hard to hear,
> I've pissed myself now I've found when I'm being
> sincere.

Fil and Guy have picked up their guitars and are playing along as Rob goes into his chorus.

> A one-night stand so far sees him through,
> I'd rather be lonely than be with you-ou…

They all pick up the tune and jam along, for five minutes or so.

'You know how you've been working on a song all day,' Rob says, 'and you just want to get it finished?'

Fil and Guy nod.

'It's hard,' says Rob.

At 7.50, finally, a car arrives at the back door of the arena with the crucial kabuki clips. To huge cheers from the audience, the front truss is lowered. Stage manager Gary stands to one side holding it steady, while Andy and a couple of members of local crew race along the line fitting the sections of spiked tube together in the purple light. 'OK!' shouts Andy and begins work on the brackets to hold the tube.

'Stand by house lights!' yells Gary. It's time for Toploader to perform, kabuki or no kabuki. Joe leads them on at a run and they launch into their first song against this background of frantic technicians. Lampey Barry has a torch in his mouth as he works. 'You'll have to excuse these people,' Joe tells the cheering crowd, 'we don't know who they are.' Big Jez is helping now, as in the newly crimson light, Andy fits the eyelets that run along the top of the curtain to the little upward spikes. Toploader launch into 'Dancing In The Moonlight'. Andy's hands twist and turn frantically as he clips the final section on and suddenly the kabuki truss is rising. Behind Toploader the huge black curtain billows lightly.

'It's up,' says Barry. 'Whether or not it will come down is another matter.'

The Boss

'We've had a few days off,' says Rob as everyone stands ready in the huddle, 'and I don't know about you lot, but it's really confused me.' There is laughter from the gathered circle. 'Coming back to do it again. I thought we'd finished – at least mentally I thought we'd finished. I've got the flu, I don't know who else has on the crew, we're in Nuremberg and we've got to do a show and we're going to fucking do it and do it well, because we do, and we do every night. So let's go out there, make them smile, think about the merchandise, more importantly make them all go home happy, because that's what we're doing this for.'

'Hear, hear!' says David.

'Now,' Rob pauses solemnly for a moment and everyone looks up. 'Who's the boss?' he asks in a totally different tone.

'You are, mate.'

And he's into the Elvis ritual. 'Go out there and be arsed!' he shouts.

'Robbie! Robbie!' goes the tape. The sold-out crowd cheers. Will the kabuki work? Wob worries. Will there be any more German nutters? worry Jonah and Marv. Will the riser be OK? worries Guy. He gets on with his worst nerves yet, tenses himself as the Terac motors haul in the six steel cords and the giant piece of Meccano climbs ever higher. Liz's blinders flash, dazzling the Nuremberg audience. Andy watches the kabuki, knuckles white with tension. It drops away, its leading edge flouncing to the floor. Like clock-work, the riser comes slowly down. Guy is grinning with relief. Gary activates the counterbalance and Rob's chair leaps up into the cage. The fans go crazy.

'Come on come on come on come on!' yells Rob. The show is back on the road.

Back at the hotel there's a bit of a sing-song. Guy's at the piano, then Claire and Joe from Toploader get up and play a bit. Fil's there too, but not at all in his normal up-for-anything post-gig mood. The bar is full of dolled-up fans as usual, but for once he finds that he's not interested. They're all a bit creepy and any attempt at a half-human conversation is getting nowhere. 'It's like "Guten Tag",' he says, 'then total silence.'

So he follows Franksy and Guy up to Franksy's for a drink. He's had enough of this groupie rubbish, he tells them. It's all such bullshit. Franksy's teasing him. 'Go on, Fil,' he's saying. 'Go back down there and try again. You're young, you're a guitarist in a well-known band, this is what you should be doing.'

Fil's not bothered. 'Yeah, yeah, whatever,' he says. He's had enough of weirdoes who can't manage more than a one-syllable answer. He's going to bed.

Five minutes go by. Fil's in the bathroom, just getting ready for bed, when there's a knock at the door. He goes over to open it and there's a girl there. 'Dressed like a porn star. Leather hipster trousers and this tiny little top. High heels. Stockings. The whole nine yards.'

Fil's resolution lasts all of one second. 'You'd better come in then,' he says.

'We've got to do a show and we're going to fucking do it and do it well, because we do, and we do every night. So let's go out there and make them smile, think about the merchandise, more importantly make them all go home happy, because that's what we're doing this for.'

The crew travel overnight to Frankfurt; the band follow by day. Rob's still got the flu, so Franksy's arranged for a medical team to give the band vitamin B12 injections, in a little room opposite hospitality. As she comes out grinning, Yolanda remembers the rush of energy she got the last time she had this shot, which wasn't at all like the energy you get from alcohol. Gary doesn't want one, doesn't like the needle, has something by mouth instead. Then he goes back to reading his Noddy Holder biography.

Fil's laughing about the way Franksy dealt with a security guard who wouldn't let the bus through the barrier into the venue. 'He goes, "Nein, nein, nein, you can't come through here," and Morris is going, "But the band, loike…"' (Fil does both German and Geordie accents.) 'And they're all just going, "Vass? Vass?" and Franksy hears it up at the top of the bus, steams downstairs, goes right up to the front, pokes his head out of the window and goes, "Hold on, hold on, ich bin das tour manager aus Robbie Williams, open das barrier, you bastard."' Fil howls with laughter. 'Open das barrier, you bastard,' he repeats.

Maybe it's the B12, maybe it's Flo's special honey tea, which Rob takes on stage with him in a plastic bottle, but his performance is better than ever tonight. He's exuberant with excess energy. He rolls on the floor. He reaches over the edge of the stage, takes the ponytail of one of the scary security guards and plays with it. He even introduces Martin the monitor engineer to the bemused crowd.

Is it because he's clean that he's doing such a stormer? Some of the fans certainly think so. 'CAN YOU KICK IT? YES YOU CAN' says a sign held up halfway back in the hall.

'In Stuttgart,' Robbie tells his audience, 'someone tried to push me off stage. If they're here tonight this is for them.' He goes into his 'You-don't-want-to-fuck-with-Ro-bbie' riff and repeats the stabbing motion, as if to a man on the floor, that he did in Paris. 'Down, sucker!' he cries.

Having laid his ghosts to rest, he relishes his power. 'Lights, please,' he commands as the lights come up. 'Off. On. Off. On.' Way back at her keyboard, Liz follows expertly. Robbie lets out a little chuckle as he launches into the next song. It's the chuckle of a man at peace with himself, utterly in control of his environment.

'Are you having a good time?' Robbie shouts, as he bounds back for the first encore section. 'I'm having a really brilliant time.' He chucks the orange towel he's carrying into the audience. As it lands, a catfight breaks out, broken up immediately by the security guard with the ponytail. Grabbing the towel, he pulls out a knife and slices it into flannel-sized sections. The fans clasp them to their bosoms.

Rob has always known he was a performer, ever since he entered himself into a talent competition in a holiday camp at the age of three. 'There was no pushy mother there,' he says, 'no parental supervision.

My mum was actually shitting herself because she couldn't find me. The bollocks on that kid! Fucking hell. It was just like, "There is the stage. I should be on that. Because I'm good at that."' He won, of course.

When he was fourteen he played the Artful Dodger in a Stoke-on-Trent production of Oliver Twist. 'It was my first lead role. And I walked out from the side of the stage, whistling and doing this walk. And the whole audience just took a breath, gasped. I physically heard them do it. I'd just won them over by walking on to the stage. They hadn't seen anything I could do yet. And I can always remember coming out for the curtain call and my cheers drowning everybody else's. I thought, I really am good at this.'

Can I Sing With You?

The flat German countryside rattles by behind the darkened windows of the band bus. Tessa leans back against the psychedelic couch of the upstairs lounge. 'Just because someone has a great voice,' she says, 'doesn't make them a great backing vocalist. You've got to understand what the job description is in a way.' It's a science in itself. 'You're not required to be the lead vocalist. You've got to have the skill to be able to blend, to be able to really use your voice as an instrument.'

She's met a lot of girls who just see it as a means to an end. 'It's like, "I'm only doing backing vocals until my solo career takes off." ' But she doesn't have any truck with that attitude; which is why she likes working with Katie. 'There's a familiarity, we don't really have to communicate about this job too much, because we're likeminded about it and it's easy.'

She and Katie have been working in a loose partnership for fifteen years. 'It's an understanding,' says Katie. 'Tessa is her own person, she does whatever she has to do, and likewise. When I'm ready to be quiet or whatever… it's fine, it works.' She laughs her wonderful laugh ('the biggest and best laugh in the world' as Rob calls it).

Both had already had long careers before they got together. Tessa has been singing since she was a girl: moving up from entertaining the troops in Northern Ireland to doing backing vocals with The Police, Bowie, Tina Turner, the Stones. As a teenager Katie worked with The Marionettes, a group who went on to tour with the Beatles. She had a solo career with her brother Mac in the seventies ('Chirpy Chirpy, Cheep, Cheep' and 'Sugar Candy Kisses' were hits) and since has sung with Van Morrison, Roger Waters, Eric Clapton.

The pair were brought in by Guy to work on some songs on the last album. Tess already knew Guy, because they'd been in the Jimmy Nail band together. 'That was funny, because Guy hated doing that gig, he wanted to be doing something else. And now he's done so well. Divine justice really, that he should do so well in the end.'

'He's a pretty strong presence, isn't he, in the whole Rob outfit?'

'Unbelievably strong. He's the captain of the ship, literally. And he steers it in a very masterful way. He's extraordinarily on top of the music side of it. But he's also really aware of the dynamic involved in being in a band. One has to get on with the boss. You can have the greatest players in the world, but if the chemistry isn't right personality-wise, it just isn't going to work.'

The chemistry works both ways.

'Rob has that ability to…' Tess pauses, seeking the metaphor to describe the effect that was first evident in rehearsal at the London Dockland's Arena. 'It's like lighting a flame underneath a burner. When he enters, even before he even sings a note, his presence is enough to just kick-start the thing into bloody hyperspace.'

'What is it about him that does that?'

'It's his energy. It's the thing that he brings to it and the thing he brings to us. He makes you want to perform. In a way, that sounds almost childishly simple. But he has that element in his make-up.

'Yet there's the paradox that Rob'll talk about not wanting to tour any more, and then he'll go on, as he did last night and have this incredible chemistry with the audience. It's as if he actually needs the audience. It might even be a chemical reaction that goes on. I think that adrenalin, those pheromones or whatever that are created from the buzz the audience gives him, are something that he needs. There's an element of it in all performers. To get where they are in the first place, there's a certain element of...' Tess trails off into another long, thoughtful pause. 'There's a void,' she continues eventually, 'that needs to be filled by this specific thing, that drives them on to do it. I don't have that void in the same way. I might have other voids, but not the one that would give me the ambition, the powerful singular drive to do it. I think it's bred by something. You'd need a psychologist to figure out what that is exactly. I don't know whether it's upbringing or whatever. But there's an element that makes them do that. That singles them out, if you like.'

Dusk

On the edge of the road, the diffuse late afternoon sun picks up skinny white-trunked birches, a lone greenhouse, a Texaco station, a tall Dutch church spire, yet more pines. It's a long drive, and the traffic worsens as we get closer to Brussels. In the first bus, Rob sleeps in his bunk. 'It's like a library on here,' Guy murmurs to David. On the band bus, Claire has also crashed. Tess and Katie chat downstairs. Franksy and Tom are working on budgets up front on the top deck. Every few minutes you hear the familiar bossa nova tone of Franksy's mobile – theme tune for the tour. Yolanda pops her head round the door of the upstairs lounge, looking for a light. 'Everyone's just spaced out,' she says.

Fil's musing about his changing attitude to the sexual aspect of rock 'n' roll. 'I've been having this little dialogue with myself lately. It's quite amusing. I was talking to someone about it the other day, I can't remember who. Anyway, they said, "You kind of come across as this good-time boy, the party lad, you're really up for it, but I get the feeling you've got a bit of a brain behind it, you know what's going on." It was like, "Yeah, of course I know what's going on." Trouble is, you get into a chicken and egg situation. It's like, If this is ironic rock and rolling, the fact is I'm actually doing it. So at what point does the irony come in? I've not really sussed that one yet.'

He's got that girl from Copenhagen coming to the gig tonight and then afterwards to stay with him at the hotel. 'And don't go writing that up as some fucking "Fil falls in love" bollocks. It's just going to be a laugh. I really like her. I'm going to have a chat and hang out with her. As opposed to not hanging out with the girl that knocks on your door at two in the morning to give you a blow job.'

Franksy's call sheet has the band arriving at the venue in 'Sproutland' at 18.00 hours. By 19.15 the bus is still stuck stationary in traffic in central Brussels. There's an accident up ahead. The blue lights of police cars flash in the dusk.

Downstairs the women are worried. It's almost going to be too late to eat before the show. Claire thinks she might plate something up for afterwards.

Yolanda's going to just dash in and have soup when they get there.

But when they finally pull up, the double door into the brightly lit interior of the Forest National is locked. It's OK, says one of the security team, they can open it. But if we go down those steps there, says Franksy, we'll have to go through the crowded public entrance, which just isn't an option.

Pompey's appeared. It's OK, it's OK, he says, in an attempt to calm the now nervy band. The stage-door entrance is this way, it's just a two-minute walk. Rob emerges from his bus with Guy, Chris, David, Josie, Marv and Jonah and everyone follows Pompey round the dark outside of the venue. It's a spooky inner-city scape, concrete pillars collaged with logo and vivid graffiti. Plenty of dark corners for weirdos to jump out of. Rough, stony ground littered with cans, takeaway boxes and other garbage. Rob's up front of the posse in his big black puffa jacket, shoulders hunched, Marv and Jonah to each side. Claire turns to David, who strides along clutching his briefcase. 'There's people behind us,' she says nervously.

It's a group of three, following. Two men and a woman. Are they journalists, fans, nutters, what? David turns and tells them to back off, showing a new and unexpectedly aggressive side. They stand where they are as the band hurries on, stumbling downhill over the dirt. No-one says anything, but everyone knows this isn't good, we shouldn't be here.

Despite, or perhaps because of, all the pre-show edginess, the gig is another stormer. If Rob has that void Tess was talking about, he's busy filling it now, strutting across the stage, keeping it sexual and personal, inviting the entire audience to be his band. All 10,000 of them should come to Berlin and sing with him, he jokes.

There is, as it happens, one man at the front who would leap at this offer. He stands tall in the middle of the girly front row with a sign saying 'CAN I SING WITH YOU AGAIN?' Rob once invited him up on stage, Franksy explains, to sing 'Angels' with him. He built a fantasy career round this one appearance, got himself a manager, started giving interviews to the press. When Rob appears after the break, he's carrying a sign saying 'NO'.

In the side-stage light of the monitor area, Franksy rocks with laughter. 'Retribution!' he shouts over the music. 'It's a tour motto.'

As Rob leaves the stage tonight, he crosses himself, something he's not done on this tour before.

Afterwards, hanging in the male dressing room with the band, Rob laughs about how he first encountered his over-enthusiastic fan. 'I was proper bored at the time,' he says, 'so I got him up on stage. He sang "Angels" and I sat by the drums. He looked like the man from Top Shop, but he did all right, he really did all right. Then he followed it up by doing loads of press. The Express, the Mail, the Star, da da da. Then he proceeded to phone up ... Josie!' Rob calls across the room.

'I don't think I've ever met anybody that was so loving as my Grandmother.

If she could have wrapped me up in cotton wool, she would have done. She gave me everything she had to give. She would have given me the shirt off her back if I'd wanted it.'

'Yeah.'

'What did he say? He phoned you up and he said …'

'He wanted to be managed, didn't he?' chips in Franksy.

Josie's laughing. 'He said could he have management and he was really pleased that all his promo had helped sell the album.'

'HIS promotion had helped sell MY album,' laughs Rob.

'And would you like to go and sing at one of his gigs – inviting you down there. Very nice.'

That's why he had the sign saying 'NO'.

'You got it upside down,' Franksy says. 'It said "ON".'

But Rob has suddenly lost interest in this story. 'I watched a David Bowie gig last night,' he says.

'From the eighties, wasn't it?' says Chris.

'Yeah, from the eighties. All he did was…' Rob slips into a David Bowie voice, complete with Bowie pauses. 'And he sang… And he looked… And he smiled… And he pointed… And he went and he sat down… For a bit… And looked at the crowd and they… Looked at him… Then he went off.'

'Fuckin' great, innee?' says Chris as everyone laughs.

'He was fuckin' great. And he didn't do anything. You know.'

'So what you're saying,' says Fil, 'is at the next gig you're going to be Bowie?'

Rob smiles. 'I'm going to get a powder-blue suit, with a white and blue tie and a shirt. I'll dye my hair blond and have it all curly on top …'

'Paint your teeth yellow,' chips in Chris.

'Yeah, and marry Iman.'

Rob picks up Franksy's call sheet and laughing, reads it out loud.

'Gary says he's down twice.'

Dabbling

Back at the hotel, Fil's with his Copenhagen girl, so there's no question of going out. It's odd, seeing him in the bar as part of a couple. Uncompetitively sure of his night's entertainment, he's happy for Tom to join him and entertain the pair of them. She's sweet, too, straight blonde hair over a smooth round face, with little blue eyes that blink open like a doll. She laughs prettily as she teaches Tom a nice thing to say to a Danish girl you've just met. 'Hi skat!' She and Fil can't stop touching each other.

Behind, at another sofa, Marv treats two young ladies to champagne. A little later, Jonah appears, then Rob. He sits with the girls for a while, then heads off upstairs with Marv. A little later, the taller, prettier girl vanishes. 'Just wait for ten minutes,' chuckles the ever-urbane Tom, 'then she follows him up. The press in the bar don't see them go together.'

'I dabbled a bit on the tour,' says Rob. 'It just depends what my frame of mind is. I've done some tours and not dabbled at all. But on this tour I put down the drink and the drugs and wanted to substitute it with something else, so I did have sex.' He smiles. 'It's allowed. I'm a pop star.

'Sexually, you can do what you want. Act out however you want to. But it's soulless. Every time you do it it's boring. It's like having a wank. But for me it's a compulsion, it was a compulsion. Sex, drink and drugs. They go hand in hand.'

'In a way,' says David, 'it's not what he wants. But in a way, he's 26 years old, for God's sake. What does a 26-year-old man do? He sleeps with women. There are all these gorgeous girls out there, waiting for him. But it doesn't give him anything. He's been doing that since he was sixteen years old. And in a way that becomes another addiction. But I'd rather he shagged some girl and worked off a bit of energy doing that. What I always say to him is, "Don't ever tell them you love them or tell them you're not leaving. Be absolutely honest about what the situation is. And if that's fine you can wake up in the morning and your conscience is clear." And don't lead them up the garden path because they want a bit of Robbie. They come in and they think they've got Robbie, but he wants to be Robert. So it's quite difficult for him.'

'Rob's a great one,' says Jonathan Wilkes, 'for finding a girl and being really keen on them for 24 hours. And he makes them feel so good they think they're the most special person in the world. Sometimes I pray for somebody to come down and fall in love with Rob. Because he'll make somebody the best husband one day; and the best dad. I know he will. But I don't think he's ready yet. And he admits that. Not for another good few years yet.'

'He does want a relationship,' says David, 'but first things first. He's got to sort himself out, which he's doing fantastically well. I'm so proud of him. Anybody at that age holding up their hand and saying "I've got a real problem here", it's the most courageous thing anybody can do. I didn't do it until I was 41. A lot of people never do it. You've got to reach a real point of pain to say, "I don't want to do this any more." When you say that, does that mean, I don't want to be an entertainer? You can think, Have I got to change everything? But what he's beginning to learn and understand is that he's a fantastic entertainer. He doesn't have to change everything, he just has to go out and entertain with his mind and his self-esteem in a different place. And he is getting some self-esteem now.'

10

'When I got clean the first time, which was for nine months, I always thought that if I kept my bed clean and if I tidied my bedroom, I'd keep my sobriety. And lo and behold, as soon as I didn't…It's a good sign for me. If my place is a mess I'm probably back to the drink.'

BE ARSED!

'And he was great! He talked to us! He say "hello".
Then we talked to him. We said the show was great.
He turned round and looked at us and said, "Yeah, I
know."' The Belgian girls outside the Conrad
International cackle with laughter as they repeat
Rob's remark. 'And we're happy because he talked to
us and he say hello.'

This lot make the hardest-bitten German fans
seem demure. They don't just want Robbie to talk to
them: 'We know he remembers us,' says Alexandra,
with a mop of curly dark hair and braces on her
teeth, 'because he's seen us a lot of times.' Even more:
'We dream to be friends with him. We dream, we
dream,' she repeats, 'so we try to make it true.'

The bus's indicators are flicking; driver John pulls
out into the traffic of Avenue Louise 71. 'Bye,
Robbie!' they shout. 'Bye, Robb–ieeeeeee!'

In Bielefeld, meanwhile, the crew are having
another drama. Caterers Mairead and Em have been
arrested. ('I didn't think their food was that bad,' says
Gary.) As usual, they'd been given local currency by
the promoter's rep in order to buy food for the day
from the local cash and carry. 'But when we handed
over the cash to pay,' says Em, 'they checked the bills

for counterfeit, as everyone does with a large transaction, and found one fake note.'

'And lo and behold,' chips in Mairead, putting on a German accent, 'ze Germans came in viz a bick gun and surrounded us and took us into a room.' She reverts to Irish. 'No, they actually gave us an apple as a gesture of friendliness.'

'Not until the end!' says Em. 'They were very feisty and strict and quite intimidating. There were seven of them, then they called the police and three policemen came. So there were ten people looking at one counterfeit note. With their gadgets. Holding it up to the light.'

In the end the promoter's rep, Mr Hartmund Ender, had to come and rescue the trapped cooks himself.

By the time Rob and the band arrive in the neon-lit dusk, the whole episode has become a huge tour joke. The menus for the evening meal have police-file type mugshots of Mairead and Em and the menu is full of jail puns.

The Bielefeld Seidenstickerhalle is not as big as the other venues. Wob has only been able to put in a cut-down set, with no riser. The relief shows on Guy's face.

Yolanda arrives in hospitality and puts on rap. Jay-Z. Volume 2. Hard Knock Life. Rob, hearing the music, walks in wearing his dark navy dressing gown, glowing with health and vigour. His eyes shine as he mimes along to the rap words, does a little rap jive. For a moment, he's from the ghetto. 'I've had it bad,' he jokes. 'I'm hard. And I like fucking women.'

Then he's off again, back to his dressing room, and Uno with David. 'Uno-flow!' he reprimands his sluggish manager, when he fails to keep up with a Skip card. A little later he's finished and back to his band's dressing room. 'Hi, I'm Rob,' he says sweetly, putting just his head round the door. 'Can I sing with you tonight?'

Before the huddle, he makes his usual little speech. 'We've had a day off. I hope it was dirty.'

'It was,' laughs Claire. 'I've had the shits.'

'We're going to go out there, do what we do,' Rob tells them. 'Be arsed!' As he runs up on stage he takes a final swig from his tea, then passes the cup to Franksy. 'Rock and roll,' he says, with an ironic grin.

It's hot in this smaller, steel-roofed venue. Up on stage Robbie is already shining with sweat after two songs. Below him the girls are fainting in droves. 'Can all the people at the front,' he announces between songs, 'can you not pass out, please.' He gurgles with laughter at his own joke. But even though the security guards hand out cups of water and douse the poor fainting nubiles with pot-plant sprayers, another and another keels over and is hoisted out from the crowd.

Robbie is also affected. His voice is going, he tells his screaming audience. 'I've got a difficult decision

to make. It's either that I perform here tonight and I don't do a show tomorrow night in Rotterdam. Or I walk off stage now and do a show in Rotterdam. Sod 'em,' he finishes, to huge applause. 'I never liked the Dutch anyway.'

Backstage, in the first break, the band members wave hands in front of faces, gulp water, wipe themselves down. Rob is concerned about his increasingly husky voice. 'I'm worried about this,' he's saying to David. 'Are they going to boo me?' David hugs him and reassures him. He's great. They're loving it. Rob doesn't know what's wrong with him. 'I've been sleeping too much,' he says.

No, says Stephan, one of the paramedic team, they didn't have more girls than usual fainting today. 'It's the same every time. People get heated up during the day and they don't drink enough.' But the paramedics don't mind coming along. Robbie's a great entertainer.

'He's got a special karma,' says Stephan, 'and he is looking to the people, looking them right in the eyes, most don't do that.'

Is that what makes the girls faint?

'No, it's the heat.'

Hard Day's Night

Later, in hospitality, Rob's voice has recovered and he's got his guitar out. Everyone sits around respectfully listening as he sings the full version of the new song he's been writing:

This is the end, I'm in pieces, I don't know what to
say,
Do you think it's best if I told her that I was gay,
I'm not really, but the truth is too hard to hear,
I've pissed myself laughing when I'm being sincere.

A one-night stand so far sees him through
I'd rather be lonely than be with you.

I'm getting homicidal tendencies, and it's insanity,
Look at the pain I've put you through.
I wanted to build for the present, for the fireside
Now I'd rather be lonely than be with you-ou.

'Nice one,' they go, when he's finished extending the
ooh-oohs on 'you'.

Chris is in best bantering mood. He doesn't want
to take a shower. 'Not in Germany, no.' He teases
Gary about the four fans who were holding up the
G, A, R and Y cards during the gig. 'Five more and
they'll have your whole name.'

As per the call sheet, the band are straight on the bus
for the five-hour journey to Rotterdam. The atmosphere is strangely flat. Fil, Tessa and Yolanda can't
decide which film to watch. They're all awful old
eighties films.

Downstairs Franksy is rolling a joint, perfectly
legal of course, now they're in Holland. The bossa
nova tone of his mobile phone keeps breaking in, as

he confers about arrival times with Rob's bus driver, chats with Josie and makes arrangements with Enrique, the manageress of the Westin in Rotterdam, who has changed her shifts to be ready to greet us at four in the morning.

The stoned check-in isn't a bad one, Franksy reckons. Sometimes it's the way to do it. 'Anything could go wrong tonight, but I've a feeling nothing will.'

The band finally crash into bed at 4.30. Tom has just fallen asleep when there's a knock at the door. Luggage. He gets back into bed and is soon asleep again. Then the phone is ringing. It's Franksy. 'Get your arse down to Level R,' he commands. 'There's some girls here and we're having a drink.'

Tom stumbles down, but there are no girls. Just Franksy and Fil, drinking vodka and tonics at five in the morning.

Around lunchtime they surface and pull back the curtains to reveal a panorama of grey. Grey sky, grey tower blocks with darker grey squares of windows. Over to the left a glass roof reveals the yellow electric light of offices. There are glimpses of desks and plants. They have, it seems, arrived in another city.

Give Me Sum

'One gig becomes pretty much like any other gig. The major difference on this tour is that I've had four great gigs in a row that I've really enjoyed. I've never been into touring before. This is the first time.

It's because I'm not drinking. It's because... a lot of fog has cleared up. I've been walking around so miserable about life and the pressure of life – and I feel so sorry for myself for having thought that way for so long. I just didn't see what a beautiful life I've got. And how lucky I am. I've worked hard, don't get me wrong, but I'm so lucky to have everything that I've got.

'I have an amazing career. Songs that people buy – and lots of people buying them. It's phenomenal. And I think it was actually that big that I couldn't see it.

'Perhaps I'm learning to like myself a bit more. It's ace. I'm enjoying stuff. I don't know why. The grace of God, probably. I pray in the morning. I've been asking for an awful lot of forgiveness just recently. Please forgive me for my thinking. Please forgive me for my... I don't know... Please forgive me for my self-pity and being blind.'

Rob was brought up and confirmed as a Catholic, but his prayers are not to that God. 'I wouldn't necessarily say Catholicism or any religious body of thought. More a power greater than myself. Put it this way, my best thinking leads me to be miserable. My best thinking leads me to taking coke when I don't want to take coke or drinking when I don't want to drink. I've come to believe in a faith, in something bigger than me. I've had it since I was a kid, really. I've been blessed. Instead of asking what I would do in a particular situation I just ask now,

"What would somebody who loves me want me to do in this situation? Or think in this situation?" Because my best thinking tells me that I'm a piece of shit. Tells me that I'm worthless, you know, which I've learnt from somewhere. And now I'm unlearning it. Teaching myself something different. I've a strong belief that a power greater than myself loves me.'

And what about something more down to earth: another person. Is he ready now for a grown-up relationship of the kind the press would love him to be having with Geri Halliwell? Perhaps even the full commitment of wife and children?

'Yeah,' he says, smiling, 'but I ain't rushing into it. And I haven't had a relationship with anybody as boyfriend and girlfriend for over two years now. The last person I walked out with was Tanya Strecker. But we weren't going out with each other, we were friends. We never committed to a relationship. She was just a nice person. And yeah, the press want to believe that I'm going out with Geri or believe I'm going out with whoever. I'm not with her. We're just really good friends.'

Does he hate the press? Over the years, with all that's been written about him, he must have got very mistrustful of men and women with notepads and tape recorders.

'Yeah, a man with a tape recorder coming in with his biased opinion about who he thinks I think I am or who he thinks I should be or who he definitely knows I'm going to be once he's written this story about me. You're pretty powerless when that sort of stuff happens.'

He looks at me more closely – a man with a tape recorder. 'Did you know anything about me before the tour?'

'I knew you were a famous pop star of the moment.'

'And what was my character, in your head?'

'Cheeky chappy. Kind of "normal", game for a laugh, everybody's best mate type of character. Those were the clichés. But you're always playing with that one, aren't you?'

'If the audience sing to me and if the audience smile, if the audience jump up and down, then I have a good time. If they don't do that then I don't have a good time. A lot of people, a lot of artists, don't want their audience to do that, they want them to listen to the music. I don't give a shit. I want them to jump up and down, smile, sing, laugh, cry. I work hard at that.

'A lot of nights I'll be looking straight at somebody and I'm not even looking at them. Because I'm scared to have contact with them. I'm scared that their reaction is going to be something that I don't want to see. It's going to put me off singing. And then other nights I don't care and I'm right with them and I love it.'

'I'm not very good in
a social environment
for conversation.

I'm getting better at it.

So the best way for me
to converse with people
or interact is if there's
something in our hands
or in our heads that
we're playing with.'

Whatever Rob's inner feelings, when he singles out a woman whilst on stage it transforms her night. At every gig there's a dazzled woman saying endlessly to her friends, 'He looked at me. He looked at me.' He must get a buzz out of that.

'It's very powerful. It works and yes, I get a kick out of it. The fact that I'm on stage pretending to be this character and that character is making that person melt. I find it: a) a boost for the ego and b) titter to myself thinking, If they only fucking knew me. If they only knew what my head does. I look at them and see who they think I am.'

'If they only knew what? That you are…?'

Rob chuckles. 'Eight,' he says, dodging the issue with a joke.

'But do you sometimes think, Jesus, I'm in control, I could do anything?'

'After songs I used to be great at ad libbing. It was always a story about shagging, drinking, la la la. But it's gone for some reason. I've burnt out in that way. I must be burnt out. It used to come so freely and quickly.'

Instead, though, Rob has been writing a lot more. And crucially, not just with Guy, but on his own. He picks up his guitar and sings his new song again. 'I'd rather be lonely than be with you-oo-oo-oo-oo-oo,' he finishes. 'I wrote a whole song! My first whole song that I've written, lyrics and music,' he adds proudly. 'I couldn't believe that I'd written the whole thing. Me and Johnny were in the flat the other night, mucking about watching Friends, and I just got the guitar out.'

'The "you" isn't anybody in particular?'

'No. Every relationship that I've been in, or that friends have been in, or are in. There's no…' He pauses, smiles disarmingly and changes the subject. 'I just couldn't believe,' he says, 'that I'd actually pieced together the chords for a verse, the bridge, the chorus and the middle eight. I couldn't believe that I'd written the whole thing. I can't even play the guitar. I don't know the chords. It's weird. I'm thinking, I've written that and if I knew a little bit more then I could write a lot more.'

Pummelled with Pineapples

Everyone seems in a good mood tonight, looking forward to two days off. Rob's going to get away from everybody for two days, skiing in Chamonix; the band are going to Amsterdam with Franksy; the crew are overnighting to Zurich, where some of them are planning a skiing excursion of their own. Jules is looking forward to red wine and canasta on the backline bus. 'Sex and drugs and rock and roll,' she laughs. Canadian Martin is just going to take it easy; he's caught the scratchy throat that's been working its way up the bunks. The other two crew buses have something altogether wilder planned, by the sounds of it.

In hospitality the band discuss the novelty of Rob continuing to be clean and in control. 'This is the weirdest tour I've ever been on,' says Fil. 'It's like people doing lines of oregano.' When the man himself appears, they all gather round, women too, for a sacred tour song: 'Ride the Punani.' They chant it over and over like a medieval choir. 'Ri-ide the Punanee-ee-ee-ee-eee-eee. Give me-ee su-uu-uum. Give me su-um Punani, give me su-um Punaneeeeee-eeeee-eeeeeeee.' After much, much laughter Rob, prompted by Franksy, goes solo with a little rap riff of his own: 'I Fuck Arse.' he sings, rising up and down the scales.

Rob is forever doing stuff like this, pointing at a man near the front during 'She's The One' and singing 'he's the one', playing with the idea of his sexuality. But has he ever really thought that he might be gay? It's a difficult question to ask.

'It's only a difficult question,' Rob replies, 'if you deem being gay as something wrong. Or dirty, or derogatory. It's not to me. It's as simple as, these men like men, these women like women, and some men like women and some men like men.'

Does his celebrity have anything to do with it? It's open season on everything else about him, so why not his sexuality, too?

'I did that when I was a kid to a lot of people in the public eye. But as a kid I would probably have been jealous. As a kid the instant thing is, "Oh, he's gay." But I'm not a kid any more. Someone said to Jonathan the other week, "Oh, I think he likes men." Of course Jonathan got upset and stuck up for me, which he shouldn't have done. I just said to him, "Next time somebody asks you if I'm gay just say, 'When Rob's good and ready to come out he will do.'" I don't give a toss if people think I'm gay.

'I wouldn't say I've not thought about it, because you do. People do when they're growing up. And I did once kiss a man in a club, but that was like – you know, your lipstick lesbians that are not really lesbians – I just walked in and there was a friend of mine there at the time and he came up and kissed me. I thought, sod it, I'll kiss you, then. But in a manly way.

'I might try it. If I was attracted to a man then I'd do it, but as it stands I haven't been physically or emotionally attracted to a man to do anything sexual with them. That's how it stands at the minute.'

If Rob is clean, the Rotterdam crowd are not. The girls in the front row pass fat spliffs to each other, take long drags, eyes closed with pleasure as they inhale. Stoned or not, they love singing. When Rob's voice fades to a croaky rasp again, they take over, the whole arena chanting 'Angels' back to him. At the end, he kneels to thank them.

Back at the hotel, Rob hosts a Uno game in the suite with the spreading view of the harbour lights below. The regulars are joined by Yolanda, Claire and a hollow-eyed record executive who clearly can't quite get his head around drinking Evian and playing a kids' card game at one in the morning.

Tom's with Fil in his room, checking out an internet site called Fil's Kilts, which was set up by a fan from Rotterdam who was in the front row tonight. 'This is really fucking scary,' Fil says. He's right. Besides fan messages of the 'feel free to worship the ground Fil walks on', 'I love Fil', etc, and the gallery of pictures of Fil pissed, Fil stoned in a bar, Fil on stage, there's a page called 'Wedding Photos'. This is a Blackpool-type picture of two people getting married in a heart-shaped frame. And superimposed on to the heads of the two people are the fan and Fil! Not content with that the fan has registered her name on the web site as Fil Eisler. So it's Fil Eisler marries Fil Eisler. 'It's just fucking surreal,' says Fil. 'I had a look at it first when I was quite pissed and stoned. A mate of mine told me about it and we downloaded it and I was just like "Aaaargh!"'

Franksy's Day Off
On the crew buses, meanwhile, they're celebrating the start of two days off after a tiring three-day run. While the backline lot play canasta and Scrabble, Liz and the party animals of the lighting bus have a beach party, with tequila all round, and all the lampeys dressed – to start with, anyway – in Hawaiian shirts. 'There was a lot of nakedness,' says Andy Jupp. 'Lots of thumping, pant pulling, trouser pulling.' At six o'clock in the morning he found himself running across a garage forecourt with one of the guys, 'both of us in our underpants, running in to buy us some

cigarettes because we'd run out. Ran up to the girl, asked her for some Marlboro, realised we only had Dutch guilders on us...Very embarrassing, both of us in our underpants as well. She wouldn't serve us.'

At some point in the small hours, creative designer Liz retired to bed, only to be dragged out and pummelled with pineapples.

'The artist has left,' Franksy announces, as he stands by the miniature lilac tree in the middle of the Westin's marble-floored lobby at lunchtime the next day, 'and I am going to get stoned as a coolabong.'

He and the band pile on to the buses and head off across the flat, green, canal-cut, windmill-strewn countryside to Amsterdam.

On Rob's bus Guy and Chris are watching a video of early clips of the band, given Chris by a fan. 'Isn't this the one where we trashed all the equipment?' asks Guy. 'Yes, yes!' goes Chris, as the TV gig ends in band-led chaos.

'Rob would love to see all this stuff,' says Guy, as lurid Europop hosts succeed each other in the OTTness of their intros. In the early sequences, Rob is so much chubbier, and looks almost lost as he sings. It's such a contrast to the lean, fit figure of today. Guy nods over at me. 'Good to see what we've been through ... This is a song Gary wrote. Gary!' They call through to the front of the bus, and the guitarist comes back and watches Rob sing his song, 'Get The Joke', which ended up as a B-side. Guy's going to make an album of the best of the B–sides and 'Get The Joke' is going to be on it. 'Nice one' says Gary, beaming.

The bus slows in the bicycle-busy streets of central Amsterdam. The hotel is across a narrow bridge, so John parks up over the canal and everyone troops across in the sunshine and through the revolving doors into the high-ceilinged crimson and gold lobby of the Hotel de L'Europe. Everyone has a room, just for the day: Mrs Bush, Mr McGigin, Mrs Mee, Mr Orff, Mr Peace, Mr Thee, Mrs Vated, not to mention those who don't require pseudonyms.

The women are going shopping, Mr Thee and Mr Peace are doing their own thing. Messrs Golseth, Orff, and Beatlate are following the round-hatted Mr Franks on a tour of Amsterdam.

They pace the canals in the lovely March sunlight and see the sights: a psychedelic coffee shop with ready-rolled joints for sale in the window. The tarts in their booths, posing in lipstick and bikini, meeting your eye as you stop to look. Just open the glass door and in you go. They're the cleanest girls in the world, says Tom enthusiastically. Checked out once a week. 'She is hot,' he says of one. 'A real Britney Spears.'

'Charlie… Viagra,' mutters a pimp on a bridge, and the gang decide that Charlie Viagra must be someone's pseudonym on the next tour. They even pay a brief and expensive call to the famous Banana Bar, where a black girl with breasts like spinnakers in a gale squats by an emaciated, 30-something blonde and says 'Shame on you!' disdainfully when the team are reluctant to ante up more than the entrance fee to receive a 'face massage'. 'Told you,' says Chris, as they leave without seeing the show. 'It's 'orrible.'

Even though it's his day off, Franksy's mobile doesn't stop ringing. Now it's Claire, who's finished shopping and wants to know where the lads have got to. We're in an Argentinian Steak House, says Franksy. Oh great, she says, she knows the place. 'What she doesn't realise,' says Franksy, 'is there's about twenty Argentinian Steak Houses in Amsterdam.' And sure enough, Claire phones back. She's in the Argentinian Steak House but we're not there. 'Told you so,' laughs Franksy. He doesn't know how to explain where we are and anyway we're leaving.

Now it's his wife Marla from London, the 'real babe' he met on the Most Debauched Tour Ever. She was supposed to be coming to join him for the gig in Zurich tomorrow, but she's just looked at her passport and realised it expires the next day. Sitting in the corner of this freak-laden Amsterdam bar, a tall beer in front of him, Franksy's not deterred. He's immediately on the case, trying to sort it with Immigration back in the UK. He is, one has to admit, the ultimate fixer.

He's doing his best, he says, to help Rob with this difficult on-tour recovery he's going through, but in the end it's David who's best in the role of sponsor.

When Rob is feeling nervous or having a moment where he's feeling low or whatever, David can help him through it, 'because he's been there, done that. For us it's very difficult. We can sit and put our arms around him and say, "Don't worry, don't have a drink," but we don't understand, because we then go and have a beer ourselves. So we don't have the experience to be able to give him that help. It's almost like having a doctor or psychiatrist on the road with you. It's great that David's his manager, because he does protect him and he does look after him. Ultimately, our main aim is – OK, we want the shows to be successful, we want Rob to sell lots of records, we want him to be the number-one star everywhere, but above that we want him to be OK. There's this thing there that people want him to be all right because we love him to bits. There's a real sense of love and concern about him. As there is in a family. We all have our madness and our crazy times, but deep down we just want him to be OK, what-ever that's going to take. Even if we would all, really, much rather do loads more shows. People like being on the road, they like touring, but Rob doesn't, so we respect that. We're not going to force him to do more than he wants to do.'

It's genuine, this love of Rob they all talk about; he seems to inspire it. Just as the fans want to take care of him, hug him, make him all right, so do the entourage.

At midnight, in various states of intoxication and

weariness, everyone finds their way back to the buses. On Rob's they're watching The Exorcist, on the band's Saving Private Ryan. On both they're using up the intoxicants that will become illegal again at the Swiss border. Franksy has finally switched off his mobile, is sprawled in the downstairs lounge with his feet up, a half-eaten kebab in his lap, and a wan smile on his face; it would be fair to say that he has achieved his declared intention of the morning.

Edgy

The band wake at lunchtime the next day to discover that they're in Zurich, outside a hotel that looks like a wedding cake, perched on the edge of a lake with misty mountains on the far shore.

At tea-time Guy decides to go for a stroll by the rippling water, blue umbrella open under the lowering grey sky. Despite his diffident manner, there is, as the band have pointed out, something quite masterful about Guy. He calls the shots, in conversation and everything else. He may ask you a question, then, halfway through your answer, suddenly turn to remark on how clean the river is.

'In the summer, I might swim in there,' he adds, surveying the clear water flowing fast under the bridge.

We stop at a little cafe where two smart couples with babies are served by a tall athletic blonde waitress in black. Swiss girls are like that, Guy asserts. Very well toned. Athletic. They go to health clubs a lot.

I haven't brought any money, but that's OK, he says. 'I'm loaded.' He gives his endearing, nervous-yet-confident smile. Who was that writer who said you need to spend money to 'oil the wheels', to keep things flowing in the world? If you hoard it up, become a miser, it blocks the flow.

So we eat costly chocolate cake and drink lattes and talk about the band, the changes that Guy has made over the past year, getting rid of one guitarist and bringing in Yolanda and backing singers Tess and Katie.

'It was totally driven by music,' he says, 'it wasn't a personality thing at all. It wasn't an easy decision. But I did it because the band wasn't funky enough. I suppose that's the biggest reason. We weren't able to play songs like "Rock DJ" with the old line-up. And I've been wanting to get Yolanda in for a while.'

Besides being very talented, he elaborates, she has an ability to ground the band. And after vocals and drums, bass is the most important thing in a band. 'If your drummer isn't good, you're fucked. And if your bass player isn't good, you're finished. You can't really get round that.'

Also she looks amazing.

'That's a great plus. I didn't – we didn't hire her for her looks. We hired her because she's an incredible musician. But that's a great bonus that she's also very sexy on stage and a good foil to Fil. What we used to have before was two guitarists running around and I used to think that was a bit much.'

So is he in charge of the band?

'Yeah, up to a point. In the end it's Rob's final decision what happens to the group. He's their boss. But I suppose I have control. Not control, but I'm the conductor of the band, if you like. I try and make sure the music is properly realised… respectfully realised. So that when people come to gigs and hear a song, one, they recognise it, because it's similar to the album and two, hopefully it's a better version of what's on the album, a more exciting version.'

Previously, Guy has talked about the immediate bonding that happened when he first met Rob. In his words, they 'needed each other'.

'We are very different, yes,' he says now. 'But we did get on from the word go. I don't really understand why, but we did. Maybe it's because he's a bit of a mirror to me in some ways, creatively. He's a reflection of, of…' Guy fumbles as he tries to find his meaning. 'I sort of… He's my voice in some ways.'

Meaning that Guy actually identifies with Rob's lyrics?

'That, and he's sung a lot of my melodies. And I was always looking for someone to sing my melodies well and front songs that we wrote together.

'The thing with Rob,' Guy continues, 'is that he is always thinking of the crowd and how they'd react to a line. And certain tricks that you can use. Like on "Rock DJ" you've got the question/answer thing. That's an old trick. But my God does it work.' It's pantomime, he adds. 'Rock and roll has always had an element of pantomime and theatre. I like that myself. I think it's fun. It might not be cool, but it's fun.

'And anyway, I think cool is a very overrated concept in rock and roll. I find a lot of stuff that's meant to be cool quite boring. People now think Abba's really cool, but when Abba was going, back in 1977, everyone thought they were trashy as hell.'

Next year, Guy's hoping to make an album for himself. 'It will be self-indulgent, yeah. I think it'll be good for me to do an album that's really personal. Just to get it out of my system. So when I come to do the next Rob record I am cleansed of musical indulgences.'

He does sometimes feel that he over-complicates the music. 'It's too clever and too fussy sometimes. I'd like to think that on the next record it will be simpler and more direct and – people use this phrase quite a lot in the music business – edgy. I tried to do it on the last album, but I don't know if I really got there.'

What would be an example of an edgy song?

'Something by Eminem, right now. A lot of American hip-hop. It's very, very… It's like a shark, it's got one function. Pop music is very particular. And I sometimes think I dress stuff up a bit.' He smiles. 'At least I'm aware of it.'

We leave the cafe and walk on, up the narrow cobbled streets, checking out the shops. 'Look at that,' says Guy, of one beautiful jewellery shop with nothing in the window but a couple of big diamond rings. Inside there are red walls and two plush crimson chairs on each side of a round table. 'I might have a room like that in my new house,' he says.

He's given up on North London's Primrose Hill and is now interested in a place in Hampstead, with views of the Heath. He particularly likes it because it's just round the corner from a scuzzy flat he lived in in his twenties when he was completely broke. 'It was just two guys sharing a room with a kitchenette on one side. We had to partition it with a piece of hardboard. I was sleeping on a single mattress with a radio, a few books and that was about it. It was pretty grim.'

Now, as we pass the specialist shops of Zurich, Guy is mentally furnishing his new place. He likes the look of that wicker sofa, this wooden music stand, that wardrobe. But cuckoo clocks are too kitsch. Well, maybe for his daughter Isis. 'Yeah, maybe.'

It was a good little tune, 'Angels'.

Rob meanwhile is staying in a private chalet in Chamonix, along with David, Josie, Jonah and Marv, and the film documentary crew. The skiing is not what everyone had hoped, blustery, blizzardy and hard to see more than five feet in front of you.

'High-class problems,' says Rob with a grin, as he

pulls off his sodden gear in the hallway. 'The skiing is awful. But the chalet's beautiful. It's somebody's house and it's obviously been here for many years.' It is, too: a chocolate-box fantasy of a place with a wooden, pitched roof, surrounded by fir trees with a view – when the snow lets up in the late afternoon – of mountains beyond.

The group stay up late, chatting and playing games in front of the hissing log fire: Dirty Little Slag again, and then another of Rob's favourites, the high-speed word association game where you sit in a circle and follow meanings: 'Blue,' says Josie. 'Sky,' says David. 'Heaven,' says Rob. 'God,' says Marv. 'Church' says Brian the documentary maker. 'Bishop' says assistant Katie. 'Fisting' says Jonah. Everyone laughs. Only Jonah could get straight from 'Bishop' to 'Fisting'. Rob rules him out, calling the shots as ever – it's no surprise when he wins. 'I'm not very good in a social environment, not very good at conversation,' Rob admits. 'So the best way for me to converse with people or interact is if there's something in our hands or our heads that we're playing with.'

Rob hasn't felt this relaxed for a long time. Everybody's getting on well. Though it's a luxurious environment, it's normal life; he's under no pressure to do extraordinary things.

Some Bodyguard's Story

Back in Zurich, the crew have bad news.

Their own skiing trip, in which twelve of them

went up by minibus to nearby Zermatt, has ended in disaster. Liz has run out of control on a too-steep slope, smashed her knee, and is now confined to a hospital bed. So lighting is going to be done tonight by her boyish assistant Rich. It is a bit scary, he says. He's seen the show maybe 50 times but he's never run it from Liz's desk and he's got to cue all the spots, which is not something he normally does.

In the large double room that is hospitality here at Zurich's Hallenstadion, the band are relaxing with the English Sunday papers. Rob appears through the door from his dressing room, wanders over to the group of sofas where the band are, slumps down on the armchair at the end and joins the gang in leafing idly through the tabloids.

Chris, meanwhile, has found a bit in the Mirror about him. '"Robbie Williams",' he reads, '"got so high on booze and drugs in New York that he collapsed in the street, pretended to be a beggar and fired a laser gun at passing cars."' He chuckles his breathy Scouser chuckle. 'It's some bodyguard's story.'

'Is it an exposé or did he sell his story?' asks Rob, matter of factly. He goes round and looks over Chris's shoulder. '"I'M THE CRACK BODY-GUARD",' he reads and puts on a tabloid reptile voice. '"We expose the minder who protects top showbiz and sports stars as kingpin of major network dealing in deadly cocaine."' He nods. It's true. He did actually pretend to be a beggar in Times Square.

'If you're being followed 24 hours a day you have no life. You're being watched. And it takes your masculinity away, because you want to go and break legs and you can't do that. It is more than weird, more than strange, to be sat in your house knowing there's four people waiting for you outside who you don't know. And as soon as you go out flashlights are going to go off, which is going to draw attention to you, which means then the road isn't safe. Then everybody knows where you live and everybody knows what's going on. And it's trauma to leave the house and to come back.'

'I was off my face. I was pretending to be a beggar and the first person that gave me any money I was going to give them £100. It was a stupid thing to do, but it was quite... freeing being a beggar.'

With which he dances away towards the connecting door to his dressing room. The press may try, he tells us, but they'll never get him down. He slams the door behind him, theatrically. He reappears. 'Aha!' he goes. No, they'll never get him down. The door closes, then – 'Aha!' – he's there again. Then he's gone. The band chuckle over their newspapers. Rob. There's a very jolly little huddle tonight. It's Katie Kissoon's birthday and Tom's downloaded one of her old songs – 'Sugar Candy Kisses' – from the internet and now plays it over the dressing-room CD. Katie shrieks with laughter and runs round the circle, pinching everyone's gonads.

Then Rob is addressing the team. 'We've all had a couple of days off, we're in Zurich, so it doesn't really matter how arsed we are.' But then, as we laugh: 'Be arsed!'

And, energised both by the break and his new, clean life, Rob sure as hell is arsed tonight. He's chattier and more full of beans on stage than he's been yet. 'It's a beautiful life, ladies and gentlemen,' he tells the wildly enthusiastic audience. 'Don't let it slip away.'

'I don't know,' he asks, after 'Better Man', 'did somebody spike my drink with drugs before the show?' He does a mad, ecstatic little dance.

'I'd like a round of applause for the lady who exposed her breasts,' he says after 'Forever Texas'. 'But if you could keep them in for the rest of the show, please.' He grins his wickedest grin. 'No, no, they're beautiful.'

'You rock, Zurich!' he shouts after 'No Regrets'. 'You know,' he adds, 'in my shows, I do have a tendency to swear and use profanities – and if that offends anybody, you can all fuck off.'

'Angel?' Robbie queries of a shouting fan below him. 'Angel? What did you call it? I don't do a song called "Angel". I do a song called "Angels". There's a definite plural. You know,' he adds over the huge cheer that greets this, 'there's two things that piss me off, well, there's more than that, but one is, "I love that song that you do, 'Angel'." It isn't fucking "Angel". It's "Angels".'

Even backstage at the end of the break before 'Rock DJ', when he sings with the hand-held mike, this over-the-top humorous energy is evident. 'Can I kick it?' he calls to them. 'I said, "Can I kick it?"' he calls, louder. He slips into a posh accent. 'I don't think you heard me. I asked you: "Can I kick it?" Well, I am coming forth to be kicked.'

'It was probably the best show so far,' he says afterwards. 'I was on fire.'

At the end of 'Rock DJ' a cake is brought on for Katie, ablaze with sparklers. 'I'd like to introduce you to Katie,' Rob yells. 'And I want you all to sing "Happy Birthday" to her. It's Katie,' he reminds them, ever the pro in the details. 'One, two, three. Happy birthday to you…'

Katie covers her face with embarrassment, first with her hand, then completely with a towel. She hugs Rob, hiding her face.

On his way back to the hotel, Rob has a bizarre encounter. Getting on to his bus after this 'supercharged' gig and going upstairs as usual, he's confronted by a portly chap with grey hair, getting out of one of the bunks in nothing but a red thong. 'I'd never seen him before in my life, so I said, "Excuse me, mate, are you on the right bus?" And he looked at me and went, "Yeah, why. Why?" I didn't know what to say, and he kept on saying "Why?" like he was going to come over and hit me.

'So I said, "Because I'm Robbie Williams and I pay your wages. Now get your clothes on and get off the bus." He was completely startled. The old bloke had got on the wrong bus. He was a driver. He hadn't got his glasses on. He'd been disturbed from his sleep and was just reacting. He kept saying, "I'm so sorry, Rob, I'm so sorry, Rob." I said, "I'm really sorry for shouting at you, man. I didn't mean to raise my voice, but you're on the wrong bus." Bless him. Red thong. Oh dear. For some reason that image has got lodged in my fantasy file.'

Rob tells this story to the long table at the postgig supper in the hotel. Then it's time to shower and change: we're overnighting to Vienna.

11

'Sing me a love song
Drop me a line
Suppose it's just
a point of view
But they tell me
I'm doing fine'

I'M ACE

There's a day off for everyone now we've reached Vienna. Josie is having a quiet mid-morning pot of tea when I find her in one of the ground-floor garden rooms of the hotel. Normally you see her active and energetic, keeping half a pace behind Rob as he goes from A to B, dancing enthusiastically alongside David on the left-hand side of the stage, shrieking with laughter. But alone she's quiet and thoughtful about her role as Rob's PA. 'You look at it all and think it's so relaxed,' she says, 'such good fun, but you're still ploughing away doing the best job you possibly can. That's what he makes you feel, that you want to do your best.

'He hasn't really ever had a normal life because he's been famous for so long. And he's done everything there is to do in a rock and roll lifestyle. He's been there, seen it and done it. He's done things that some of us will never do. Now he's reached the stage where he just wants to live comfortably and quietly. He loves his sport. But all the things that his job gives him access to, he doesn't want. He doesn't want to be flown out to Milan by the Versaces to sit in the front row of a fashion show and be given free clothes. He doesn't want to go to a nightclub where all the drinks are free. He doesn't drink. He's just grown up, really, I think.'

So he just wants a nice quiet life?

'Of course he does. He wants to have a great house and a wife and kids. It's possible, of course, but it's difficult for anyone to find their partner in life, isn't it? Even more so for him, because he's very limited as to where he can go to meet people.'

And you must always wonder who your real friends are.

'Yeah.' But he has got real friends. More so, this year, in the last few months. A few people close to him he can trust, rather than a huge entourage of 50 willy-nilly friends. He's got his flatmate, Jonathan. Josie names a couple more.

But you can never lie to Rob. Or be anything other than completely honest or straight up. You can't pull the wool over his eyes, because he is absolutely aware of everything going on all around him. He might not say anything at the time, but a few days later he'll refer back to something and you'll be absolutely amazed. 'He'll mull things over. He hasn't got a temper; he doesn't blow up. He's an interesting and complicated little thing.'

'I love Josie,' says Rob, 'but I don't think she would regard me as a friend. I would do anything for her. If she didn't work for me, I'd class her as a friend. But I don't think you can class people that you pay as friends. Apart from David Enthoven. I don't think you can put them in that category. You can't be friends with somebody that is there at your beck and call. She's all give and I'm all take. But that's her job.'

'Josie has to be this little Rottweiler,' says Jonathan Wilkes, a close observer of the intimate interaction between Rob and his PA. 'She has to take a lot of shit and she's brilliant at her job. I can't think of anyone else who could do it. Basically, she's got to cope with Rob. His demands at work, everybody else's demands from him – she doesn't stop working. Josie's boyfriend is Robbie; her life is Robbie, bless her; and I think she deals with it so well.'

Fil and Rob are jamming in hospitality when the record company people come in with the awards. First off, it's the local company, to present the first gold record from Austria for some time. Then it's Tony Wadsworth, chairman of EMI, London.

'This is the big one,' he tells the gathered group, confidently. 'I'm not one to denigrate the Austrians' achievement, which is huge, but we thought we should do something to recognise the fact that this album has sold more than four million copies around the world…'

EMI have made a map of the world, with Robbie's record sales marked. 'So you can see all the places and how you've been selling…'

'Have I gone gold in Mexico?' asks Rob, studying it.

'Yeah.'

'Singing "Re-light My Fire" is just a cheap gag that people laugh at. I don't mean to be offensive to the other boys that were in Take That. I genuinely don't. But a lot of the times when you're on stage you just struggle to find something funny to do or say. And it's always been a mainstay of what people laugh at. And I'm not rehashing the past or being bitter about the past. It's just a cheap gag that maybe I should stop doing. But it gets a laugh.'

'The success of this album has been incredible,' Tony continues. 'Nobody apart from the Beatles sold more albums in the UK last year…'

'Who?' says Chris.

With yet another load of people focused on his reactions, Rob is modest and grateful.

'Thank you very much, Uncle Tony. I'm so chuffed, I really am… It's so great.' He looks down at the chart and starts chanting. 'Spain, gold. Sweden, gold. Canada, gold. Hong Kong, gold. New Zealand, platinum times five…'

There's a cheer from the gathered throng.

'More records than sheep,' says Rob.

'The sheep are buying it, yeah.'

Rob's going faster: 'Arabia, gold. Australia, gold. Ireland, platinum times ten. Singapore, gold. Denmark, platinum. Holland, gold. Mexico, gold. Germany, platinum. Belgium, gold. Thailand, platinum. I haven't been there either. See!' He looks over at David. 'You don't really have to go. You can cancel all those television shows. Austria, gold. Switzerland, platinum. Italy, platinum. Chile, silver. UK – oh yeah – platinum times seven.' He nods. 'That's really cool.'

Everyone claps.

But Rob's thinking there should have been more platinum. 'Honestly,' he says later. 'I thought it was amazing, but I have a disease of wanting more more more. I was thinking, Mexico, gold. Why's it only gold? I've never been there, so yeah, it probably should be gold, but why shouldn't it be platinum? I think we all suffer from the disease of wanting more. Never happy with what we've got.'

'A round of applause,' he says now, gesturing over towards the EMI people. 'Guys, thank you very much for all your hard work.'

'Thank you.'

It's another storming gig tonight and Rob's riding high. The tour's nearly over, he's still clean, and he's actually, for the first time in his life, enjoying himself on stage.

'To-o-o-uch me, take me to that special place,' he begs the crowd, knee up on the monitor, leaning back, left hand swinging. 'I'm doing all I can…' he croons, then puts his hand up to his ear. 'To be a better man,' they yell back. 'This is "No Regrets",' he announces. 'By me! Robbie Williams!' Out come the lighters. Thousands of people sway from side to side in the flame-dotted darkness.

> Sing me a love song
> Drop me a line
> Suppose it's ju-u-ust a point of view
> But they tell me I'm doing fi-i-ine

'And I am!' shouts Robbie. 'Vienna – I'm doing great!' He punches the air.

'A man came up to me from Manchester,' he tells the ecstatic crowd, chatty as anything again, 'and said, "Robbie, how do you do it? How do you make such brilliant songs?" He did. All right, then, he said,

"How d'you make such half-decent songs?" He said, "You're so good-looking and you sing so well." ' Rob laughs delightedly at his own ad-libbed story. 'And I said, "Flattery will get you nowhere." And he said, "Please, do me a favour, will you write a song for me?" And I said, "Yeah, yeah, I'll write a song for you, but you've got to promise that you don't tell anybody that I wrote it." And he said, "All right, then." And the song goes like this.' With a gurgle of laughter, he launches into the Gallaghers' 'Wonderwall'.

Backstage in the break they're all bright-eyed and excited. Rob hugs Fil and kisses Yolanda. 'The atmosphere is electric tonight,' says Josie, eyes shining.

'I was speaking to the band backstage,' Rob tells his audience, 'and they were just saying this is one of the best, if not the best show I've ever done.' He stands with his fist triumphantly clenched in the air. 'I'm truly speechless,' he adds, after 'She's The One'. 'I'm truly overwhelmed by you all tonight.'

'Ladies and gentlemen,' he concludes, after a supercharged 'Rock DJ' finale, 'you have been the best fucking crowd I've ever had.' He stands there shaking his head, tears in his eyes as he looks out over the mass of faces. 'You've made a grown man cry.'

In his dressing room, he slumps back on the sofa with a guitar in his hand. 'I can't describe what that was like,' he says. 'I knew it was going to be good, right from the start. I was sure of it. When I came on I just felt so free and I couldn't put a foot wrong. They lapped it up and they loved it. That was one of the highlights of my life, ever. It was the loudest crowd, the best crowd, the most responsive, and I performed really well. I was loose, relaxed, made all the right moves. I don't know what my singing was like because I wasn't concentrating.'

He smiles and shakes his head as he looks round at us. 'I didn't want this tour at all. I didn't want to do this year. And now it's going to be so weird come November when it all stops. So many nice things happening to me. I just failed to see them for so long. I had my head stuck firmly up my arse. No shit. Self-pity, self-pity, self-pity. I failed to see all the great things about my life and there are so many. And I feel so sick that I haven't seen it before. I really do. But I'm 27 and it's a nice time to see it.

'There was no doubt that I was going to get on stage tonight and have a good time. I just felt it in my bones. I think they detected that. Because if they see you're having a good time, they feel as though they're part of that, which they are, they're so part of it. If they see you smiling, genuinely smiling, they love it. They love it. Because they're proud that their town, them as people, have made you smile and enjoy yourself. You saw it when I said, "This is the best gig I've ever done." They just went, "Yes." I'm just getting better at it.

'I'm not going to say I love you all, but I love most of you. This is the end of my tour, I've had a great time, and I can't wait to see you again. Please come back and see me next time. If you've liked my show I'll be Robbie Williams, if you haven't liked my show I'll be Craig David. Good night.'

'It was an out-of-body experience. There was so much love being aimed at me. Just being thrown at me by thousands of people. They were all genuinely pleased to see me and genuinely happy that they'd come to the gig. And all sang along and all put their arms in the air. Just that concentrated love being thrown at me. 13,000 people.' He looks over at Josie with an incredulous look. 'I'm on stage going, "I'm ace." And there's 13,000 people going, "We agree."' Josie shakes her head and shrieks with laughter. 'What is better than that?' Rob asks. 'What could be better than that?'

Outside, the Austrian royal family is waiting to meet him.

When the performers have all gone, hospitality slowly fills up with disgruntled crew: their view of the gig is dictated by the fact that they've got a famously shit local crew, who are a) stupid and b) off their gourds. Dave Bracey has a very different perspective on the show from his ecstatic boss. What is Rob up to? It was the worst vocal performance he'd heard in ages, worse than Zurich, which he thought sounded like 'a bag of spanners; it just didn't lock together for me at all'. As for Rob's microphone technique, a child could have done better. He's wondering whether he should say something. 'I never go out of my way to tell him I think something's crap, but perhaps I should.' It's a fascinating divergence of opinion between the expert sound technician, who has spent his life bent over knobs and dials trying to mix the perfect assonance for the audience, and the rumbustious performer, who reacts to and is impressed by something far more visceral. 'I don't know what I'm listening to,' Rob admits cheerfully. 'I haven't got a clue. I must be the easiest front man ever to work with. I don't know what goes up, what goes down, what should be here and what should be there. I just sort of muddle through.'

The Reluctant Pop Star

Where are we now? Oh right, Munich. Another grey German dawn, another venue, another gig, the second from last. Production, riggers and catering haul themselves blearily from their bunks. 'It's a beautiful day,' sings Mairead, as she hoists a box of fruit out of the pink flight cases marked 'Popcorn Catering'. 'Don't let it slip away… Six years in college,' she adds as she swigs black coffee from a polystyrene cup, 'training to be a chef. What the feck am I doing here? But I like the time off. I go to my house in the Bahamas and I just chill…'

On the wall of the kitchen a note has been pinned up.

'GRAHAM MORRISON IS A CHARLIE
BIG BANANAS.
WHEN HE SOLD HOT DOG 'N' ONIONS
HE CALLED ME ALL THE TIME. NOW
HE DOES ROBBIE HE

BLANKS ME (VIENNA).YOU WILL BE BACK
WORKING IN FAIRGROUNDS IF YOU
DON'T WATCH OUT.'

Graham is laughing as he unpacks his pots, pans and
utensils. This was an old mate from home, now on
Tom Jones's crew, whom he just didn't get time to
meet up with in Vienna.

As the truck drivers stroll down, whistling, for
their breakfast, Mairead's planning today's shopping.
How many fillets of beef will she get for the beef
stroganoff? Four, Graham thinks. Then it's off with
Em and the local runner to the huge Metro cash and
carry on the edge of town.

'Get a trolley, flower,' Em says to the skinny
German with the leather trousers and flat cap. 'You're
with me.'

Mairead flies around the aisles, loading up with
everything from seafood for lunch to chocolate fingers for Rob's bus, stealing boxes where she can. It's a
bizarre feature of German supermarkets, she
explains, that they don't give you boxes to take your
shopping away in. And 2756 Deutschmarks later, the
pair are in the minibus, racing back to get started on
dinner.

Catering is the heart of the tour, Em thinks.
'Because you can get your physical nourishment, but
hopefully you can get some sort of emotional support as well. "Have you got a bit of chocolate? I'm
having a bad day." You can just come in and there's

usually somebody in the catering department who you can hopefully get comfort from.'

It's like a pseudo family, the touring community. 'The dynamics within the family are the same as with any other family. You don't have to get on with everybody, but there's a tremendous tolerance of idiosyncrasies amongst people. The stick is awful, but there's tremendous loyalty as well. But if you've got a slight Achilles heel, that's it, it's going to be exposed, but more often than not it's not a spiteful thing. You'd do it to your brother, so you're going to do it to the person sat on the bus next to you.'

That evening, fortified by a plate of Mairead's beef stroganoff, Rob is on ace form again. 'Let's face the Munich and dance!' he tells the band in the huddle. 'Scheize,' he tells the crowd, pointing at himself. 'Brilliant!' He points at them.

Though it's the last night of three, it's quiet on the fabled lampeys' bus tonight. There's no beach party, no tequila, no drugs – just wine and beer and the conversation of the weary. Your body always knows, says lighting crew chief Mark England, when you're getting to the end of the tour. You get the kind of lurgey he's got now. 'On a really long tour you get two weeks of it.'

We talk about Rob, of course.

'I think he's the reluctant pop star,' says Mark. 'I feel he'd like to be a normal person and he can't. I've worked for a lot of bands and I've seen what being a star can do to you. I've seen band members have mental breakdowns, have drug overdoses, get into weird sexual stuff. I think anybody who can be a star and deal with all the adulation and come through it and still be a decent human being and keep their mind together is doing really well. And Robbie is a lovely geezer, down to earth, but I think he would just like to be an ordinary person.'

'It's one of the few industries,' says George with the hat, 'where no-one aspires to be the boss.'

New Millennium

Two nights later, back in Rotterdam for his final gig, Robbie's like a man possessed. 'I've come to entertain you – you – you – you – you!' he begins. He stands there like Kitchener in the famous old war poster, pointing out into the audience. He jumps, fist in the air, and swaggers across the stage like Sinatra. Closes his eyes and breathes deeply. Bends politely to talk to the front row. Works the crowd: 'The front row, how yer doing? The second row, how yer doing? Everybody in the back, how yer doing?' Fucks up the opening of 'She's The One' and turns it into a joke: 'What we're going to do is, I'm going to go off, then I'm going to come back on like you've not seen me.' Brings up Take That: 'I used to be in this band that played here once. What we used to do is something like this – "Re-light my fire, cos I need... your love".' Takes his trousers down. Praises his audience: 'Wow! You sound good tonight. I'd like to take you back and shag you all. Guys included.' Gets them jumping during 'Kids'. And their hands up for 'Millennium'. They all sing 'Angels' for him. 'I sit and wait...After you,' he says politely.

You know it all so well now, but it's still extraordinary. The sight of 10,000 arms waving brings tears to your eyes again. And as he launches into his 'Rock DJ' finale there's a set-piece surprise, as the entire crew, dressed in pink, blue, green and crimson curly wigs, come leaping on to the stage like a horde of muppets, dancing up and down the set they've built from scratch, today and every day, lining up at the back of the set to give the gig, the tour, a pantomime finale. At their centre, is the old bus driver who challenged Rob after the Zurich gig, naked except for his red thong.

Robbie turns, thoughtful as ever, and beckons them down. 'Come and take a bow,' he calls.

'Ladies and gentlemen,' he tells the audience, 'I'm not going to say I love you all, but I love most of you. This is the end of my tour, I've had a great time, and I can't wait to see you again. Please come back and see me next time. If you've liked my show I'll be Robbie Williams, if you haven't liked my show I'll be Craig David. Good night.'

'Lord. Lord, Lord, Lord,' he mutters, as he sinks back on to his dressing-room sofa. 'I'm over the moon. Got through the tour. I'm just really comfortable and I'm just really enjoying my life, really enjoying the fact that all those people out there enjoyed themselves tonight, and you know, I enjoyed myself, too. For the majority of the tour. It's only a couple of nights I didn't like. One being Sweden, the other being wherever it was it doesn't really matter. Now it's the difficult time. For me. As an alcoholic. It's like there's always a reward. A reward for doing something and a reward for, you know, finishing the tour and doing well and being a good little pop star. You know, now is the time I normally reward myself with five grams of coke and as much booze as I can stuff down me gullet. Just have to remind myself that I don't need to do that now. Because it's all going to kick off now around me. Because everybody's worked really hard and I'm probably the only alcoholic, drug addict on the tour. So everybody that works for me now goes and gets pissed. I go back to the hotel, have a cup of tea and play some Uno. And that'll do for me.'

'Is that really OK?'

'Yeah. It really is. It really, really is. You know, I don't want to drink. That hasn't stopped me in the past from putting it down me neck. Good luck to 'em. I'll see 'em tomorrow with hangovers.'

Rob's right. Back at the Hotel de L'Europe the band gets satisfactorily trashed. In the corner of the bar, Guy plays superior cocktail piano. Rob appears for a short while in his woolly hat, then he's off upstairs to the Evian and the Uno table. Much, much later, in

Tom's room, watched by the three girls from Dusseldorf (visiting by arrangement) and Franksy's wife Marla (who is a babe), Fil attempts to throw a TV out of the window, but is restrained by the tour accountant, who points out that he'll only have to pay for it later, dude.

Truly this is rock'n'roll for the new millennium.

12 RW

'If I wasn't Robbie Williams right now, I'd probably be auditioning for the Big Brother household.'

TURNAROUND

The Sermon On The Mount tour is over, and Rob has returned to London, the Kensington Park Road flat, and the person who probably knows him most intimately these days, best friend and flatmate Jonathan Wilkes, five years his junior. 'Since I came flying out of my mum's womb, he was there,' says Jonathan, lyrically. 'His green eyes were sparkling at me. Rob was like my big brother. I always remember looking up at him, because you do, you tend to find a role model in life, look up at an older boy and think, I want to be him.'

Jonathan is realistic about the part he played in Rob's life when they were kids. He wasn't old enough to be one of the big boys. 'They would try and involve me as much as they could, but I was always the little shit that got in the way. He was horrible to me, but I used to be a right nuisance.'

'He was a little twat,' Rob confirms. 'I used to beat him up regularly.'

Things have altered radically, however, now they've both grown up. During Rob's time in Take That, Jonathan was still in school, but when he moved to London at eighteen, Rob suggested he stay for a week while he found his feet. 'So I did,' says

Jonathan, 'and I ended up staying four years.'

The roles changed. Rob, says Jonathan, 'was in his full prime of drinking, of drugs. I became the big brother, the one looking out for Rob. When Rob would start drinking, I would stop drinking to look after him; when he'd start taking drugs I'd pre-warn people not to give him drugs. It would come to the end of a party and I'd be walking round saying to people, "Please don't give any to Rob, please don't." '

'He was helping me out,' says Rob, 'by the very fact that he was there and he was somebody that I trust and love. I don't think you can physically force anybody to react in a certain way, but it was just his presence there that made my life easier; he helped me and he got me out of lots of scrapes.'

Now Jonathan reckons they're closer than brothers. 'It's quite frightening. People say when they meet us, "God, you two absolutely love each other, don't you?" It's true. We need each other. I can say that. It's not a cheesy or corny thing to say. He misses me if he's away. He said that if he had his way he'd have me with him twenty-four hours a day.'

Part of this mutual reliance undoubtedly has to do with the fact that, in a world full of people eager to have a piece of him, Rob can be totally normal with his old Stoke mate, and vice versa. 'I sometimes don't realise how big he is,' Jonathan says. 'People talk about him and I think, Shit, he's that big, he really is that big. I get confused sometimes and I think, He's just Rob who I live with. And I'm probably the only

'It's like I've been in this deep sleep, this deep nightmare and I've just woken up and seen how great things are.

It is a complete 360° turnaround.'

one in Rob's life who can tell him to fuck off; who can say, "Oi! You're being a bit of a prick here."' Everyone else in Rob's world, Jonathan reckons, is part of the Robbie Williams empire.

Not that Jonathan isn't a fan. He's Rob's number-one fan, talking about him as 'the biggest thing in our country', 'into the phenomenon stage', 'the best entertainer this country has ever produced'. Even though he's just launched his own pop career, Jonathan has nothing but admiration for his friend. 'Somebody asked me, "D'you get jealous?" I'm like, "God, no. Not at all." I'm so fucking proud of him.'

Yes, there was a little frustration that all the journalists interviewing him about his first single, 'Just Another Day', only seemed to want to know about Rob, but that's their problem. And Jonathan has been well able to deal with them. 'I said, "Look, I'm not going to give you anything – this is about me. You're interviewing Jonathan Wilkes here." Then they'd turn it round and say, "Well, who does the washing up?" I'd say, "For God's sake, that's a really shit question." In the end I used to say, "I'm not answering that." They all wanted to know the Robbie Williams connection. There even used to be some stupid talk about me and Rob being gay. Two boys who live with each other. We're just two mates from Stoke-on-Trent who've been friends all our lives. Get a life.'

Weddings, Bar Mitzvahs, Stadiums

Despite his worries of the last night of the tour, Rob is managing to remain clean. He's going regularly to his self-help meetings and facing his demons one day at a time. Jonathan noticed the change as soon as his friend returned. 'He came back a different person. He said, "Johnny, I fucking love my job. I loved the tour." Rob not drinking is a different person,' he adds. 'When Rob drinks he turns into someone that I don't know: a slag; an aggressive, rude… He hasn't got any sense of humour, no appreciation of life.' Sober Rob on the other hand is 'clever, funny, intelligent, creative, charming… he's got all this going for him. That's why he can't drink any more. Because the thing doesn't agree with him.'

Rob agrees with this assessment. The sense of a new perception of his life, which he was gradually discovering on tour, continues. 'It's like I've been in this deep sleep, this deep nightmare and I've just woken up and seen how great things are. How wonderful my job is and what a gift it is. How lucky I am as a 27-year-old, to be given everything that I've been given. To be able to do what I'm doing. I sound like I'm gushing saying it, but it is a complete 360-degree turnaround from where I was seven or eight months ago.'

Happy at last with his lot, Rob continues to do the things that career pop stars have to do to keep the ball in the air. He flies to Paris with the band on a private plane to do a TV show, Tapis Rouge. Waiting around beforehand, he gives the twenty or so fans gathered at the back door of the studio the kind of Robbie moment that makes their long vigil worthwhile, as he dances out into the yard with his guitar, wearing nothing but a pair of tight black Speedos. And even though he's faced inside with a seated, sedate, largely middle-aged crowd, he uses his old showman's tricks to get them going (a little), telling one side they're clapping out of time, while making the thumbs-up sign to the other; giving them the old one-to-one eye treatment; slipping into French as he sings of trying to find 'l'amour suprême'; sitting on a girl's knee and kissing her; going over to shake the hand of a cute little boy in the front row.

A few days later he turns up at an industry awards ceremony in London's West End, to thank the gathered radio professionals for his 'amazing, amazing life'. He's aware, he tells his appreciative audience, that the majority of his success is due to radio, to people listening to records and then going out and buying them. In the past he never used to turn up for events like this, 'Because I thought, sod 'em, I'll not win next year, they can all sod off.' But now, winning for the third year running, he's as humble, unhubristic and grateful as he was at the Brits. 'I don't know how long this lasts for,' he says (and note his fatalistic use of the present tense), 'this run or this roll that I'm on. But thank you everybody that supported me in radio. You put me where I am.'

Then it's on in the limo to Sotheby's, for the launch of an auction of private gear from the

Notting Hill flat, which he's soon to move out of, in aid of the charity Give It Sum (which Comic Relief administrate and which has just donated over £200,000 to projects in the Stoke area alone). Most famously, of course, there's Rob's bed, on which he sings the single word 'Mammaries' to the tune of 'Memory', to much laughter, before making a hurried two line speech and heading home.

The next day there's another private plane, bouncing scarily through the windy sky to land (just) in Manchester for an afternoon-long appearance on the Mark and Lard show. Rob tells the identically dressed Radio One hosts how he's auctioning 'beds, pants, aunties, family, just stuff I don't need any more' and answers all the familiar questions about Geri, not drinking and the upcoming stadium tour, as well as some unlikely new ones e-mailed in by listeners:

'Does the tattoo on your left arm have a specific meaning, because my mate Dave says it's just a basic Maori pattern, but I heard it was your life story in hieroglyphics?'

'It's a basic Maori pattern, but it fits my life story which is basic Maori, which is not bad, really, for someone from Stoke-on-Trent.'

'What's your favourite pasty filling? Mine is cheese and onion.'

'Chicken tikka.'

'What's your favourite type of cheese?'

'Don't eat cheese. Causes a lot of phlegm build-up in the back of me throat.'

'It's a beautiful day, don't let it slip away.'

'These are the things people want to know,' says Mark. 'Amazing revelation and insight.'

As Rob leaves the studio and walks down the long corridor of the BBC building, people keep popping out of doors asking for autographs. Outside, even at the back of the building, the car is chased by yet more signature hunters. In the private plane, the captain turns round mid-flight. 'I'm awfully sorry, this is terribly unprofessional, but my kids have been bothering me something rotten. Would you mind…?'

The next afternoon Rob's on Parkinson, with Hugh Grant. It's another long wait between afternoon rehearsals and evening transmission, and then the Great Interviewer launches into his own version of the mantra. 'Big headline in the paper: "He's in love with Geri"?' 'What about the booze and the drugs and things?' 'You're selling your bed?' Rob flashes the double dimples and trots out the well-rehearsed answers.

Backstage, afterwards, Robbie runs into Jeremy Paxman and they have a celebrity moment in the corridor, as the entourage stops to watch. 'Nice to meet you,' says Rob. 'Are you going on next?'

'Sorry, not grand enough. Off to grill a minister about foot and mouth.'

'Give 'em hell.'

Then Hugh appears in Rob's dressing room (alarmingly like he is in the movies) introducing, 'Er Sarah, er, a girl who works in my office, a huge, huge fan…'

As spring turns to summer and Rob stays clean, he moves out of the Notting Hill flat into a house in Chelsea, a decompression chamber before he takes up residence in the big new house with the pool table and the giant fish tank in the nameless part of London where fans will undoubtedly track him down sooner or later.

Jonathan moves with him and is glad to see the back of the old place. 'It was horrible,' he says now. 'Like a goldfish bowl. Especially now when Rob's not drinking and has turned a corner. You look back – all the memories that are in that place. I can remember the times when there was a pile of cocaine there and I've just sat up till eight in the morning while Rob's done this pile. I haven't touched it and I'm nodding off and it's breakfast time.'

Sobriety isn't the only change in Rob's life, though. After a ten-day trip to the South of France to shoot a short film, he reflects on a changing attitude to sex. 'When I took drugs,' he remembers, 'I'd end up every evening in the toilets trying to shag people. That's embarrassing. Really seedy. Well, not seedy, but I just wanted to have sex, compulsive sex. That saddens me.'

Now he's quite enjoying going to bed alone. 'I went to a club in the South of France,' he says, 'and it was amazing. I was sat in that club and I was looking round the dance floor for the glazed-eyed pillock that was nil by mouth, hanging outside the girls' toilets, and I couldn't find him, because there was only me. That evening there were a lot of pretty girls dancing and flirting. I went and chatted to a few and then it was time to go home. I was walking down the street thinking, That's surreal. I've always been intent on pulling somebody and now I just want to go home and be by myself.'

But not totally by himself. There's a new companion, a little Rottweiler puppy. 'D'you know what it was called?' he says with excitement as he comes back from his first meeting with the dog. 'She's The One. Before they even knew it was me turning up to see it. And its father was called Mr Bo Jangles, which is one of my favourite songs. "Mr Bo Jangles, Potters Pride."'

He's looking forward, he says, to the responsibility of having another life in his life, 'and becoming really good mates with this little girl.'

And there's another development. He's decided to buy a house near to his new house – for his mum. 'I can't wait for her to be there,' he says, 'because I want to wake up in the morning and go round to my mum's for breakfast, or my mum come round to mine for breakfast. It's such a great place to be for me, because I just didn't want that six months ago.

'When I took a lot of drink and drugs, you go into therapy and they tell you it's all your parents' fault. Then if you relapse, all you're left with is, It's your parents' fault that you're still pissed. So you get very angry at them. I've always had the strongest ties with my mum, because I love her. And it's been very painful for us both these last three years. Because I've just been pissed and resentful and didn't want the responsibility of her or my sister or anyone else being around me, because I didn't know how to handle them. And I didn't know how to deal with these feelings of anger towards people. But they've all subsided. And I'm getting the most amazing relationship again with Mum, like I had before I joined Take That, or while I was in Take That. We speak daily.

'We chat and we're friends and she's my mum and she can give great advice and she's loving and caring. I used to be coming down off coke, or coming down off booze, I used to try and find a happy place, and I just couldn't, there was nothing. I used to try and think of my family and I felt like an orphan. And now I do have that family back. I do have a parent. I'm not alone.'

'Was it the recognition you were after, rather than the fame?' I ask, as we sit in the garden of the Chelsea house one evening shortly before the start of the summer stadium tour, 'Weddings, Bar Mitzvahs, Stadiums' Franksy has christened it. 'It's not as if you're like the Hear'say people, just wanting fame.'

He grins. 'I'm a member of Hear'say,' he replies. 'I am. I wanted to be bigger and better. I wanted a dream. Whether that's fame or recognition or being good at a certain thing. When I stepped out for the curtain call of the Artful Dodger, my cheer was louder than anybody else's and that felt good. In a different set of circumstances, if I wasn't Robbie Williams right now, I'd probably be auditioning for the Big Brother household. I would. Because I wanted to bigger and better myself. I wanted that dream. Some people's dreams are different; I think a huge majority of people's dreams are the same. They want to be bigger, better, they want the glamour, the fame, the celebrity.

'I got it at such an early age, such an impression-able age. I think every fourteen, fifteen, sixteen-year-old thought like me in some sort of way. I'm going to be famous for something. People do. But I got it. I got it really early with Take That. It was something that, at the time, I felt ashamed of and didn't want to be famous for, but it was my only route in. I'd have been happy doing fucking anything then to make myself famous.

'I just wanted people to like me, basically. But on a grand scale. On a huge scale. The world has to adore me – or had to adore me.'

And now they do.

'They do. I've got what I wanted.'

And was it worth it?

'I'm still learning to cope with it. Be careful what you ask for...' He leans back, eyes shining as he smiles his famous smile.

'Because you might just get it.'

13

'Come and hold my hand,
I want to contact the living
Not sure I understand
This role I've been given …'

SWINGING WESTWARD

Rob's eyes are tight closed as his lips croon up to the flat microphone shield. His brow is as furrowed as it ever was when he was singing from the heart. His hair is wilder, though, his skin browner. He's visibly fitter and musclier in his white T-shirt with the crimson and black trim and the Gorillaz logo.

It's a year later and he's back in the studio, recording a new album. He never really did have that year off, though he's not been doing much except writing and relaxing these last few months. And moving to America, of course. This studio we're in is in Los Angeles, where Rob has bought a house and is now living full time.

'That was fucken wicked,' he says, when the verse is finished. He looks up from the microphone and laughs. 'Here you can see the artist in his natural habitat,' he jokes, 'during the Middle Eight, when he hasn't got anything to do. Just relax and sway with the band, like so.' He dances a little. 'Watch him as he thinks of breeding,' he adds, in a David Attenborough voice. 'Watch him as he fucks up and comes in at the wrong place because he's not concentrating. Watch him as he struggles to hit the high notes. Watch the team in the studio not caring so much because of the marvels of computers …'

Rob's cue comes up and he gets back to work.

'I just want to feel real love,' he sings.

'In the home that I live in …'

'That's it,' he says, when the song – 'Feel' – is finished. 'Now we press it. Mix it tonight. Goes in the shops Tuesday. *Top of the Pops* Thursday. Number One by Saturday. Yacht by Sunday.'

He wanders off, out of the vocal booth and into the main studio, where friends and management are there to applaud and support. Best mate Jonathan Wilkes, girlfriend Rachel Hunter, manager David Enthoven, PA Josie Cliff (not to mention Rob's new trio of dogs: Rudy the Alsatian, Sam the Labrador-Pit, Sid the Wolfhound). Up at the monitor desk are Rob's long-term producer Steve Power and veteran A & R man Chris Briggs. Standing by their instruments are Rob's producer: Guy Chambers and fellow musicians: Gary Nuttall (looking unchanged in a pressed white short-sleeved shirt), Jeremy Stacy on drums, Phil Spalding on bass and Neil Taylor on guitar all chosen by Guy. 'This reminds me a bit of the first album,' he says. 'I think it's got the energy, because we're all playing together in a room, Rob's buzzing off that, and I think it's got some of the youthful energy that the first record had. So I'm very excited, because I wanted it to go in that direction anyway.'

Will the new album break America, as everyone

hopes? Guy is sagacious as ever. 'If Rob wants to it will,' he says. 'It all comes down to that really. It's just whether he wants to put in the enormous effort that is involved in breaking the States. You're looking at six months minimum – of touring. For an artist like Rob that's the most important factor, because when people see him live – they get it.'

Rob is in an equally upbeat frame of mind. 'We've recorded four songs in two days,' he says, as he drives off with Jonathan Wilkes to the house he's rented from Dan Ackroyd up on Mulholland Drive. 'And there's four Number Ones. It's just fucking huge. It's going to be the best album I've ever done. It's going to be the one I've always wanted and' – his voice modulates into a mock-posh accent – 'I ain't going nowhere. I can't be stopped, because it's Bad Boy for life. *Aight.*' He makes a noise not dissimilar to his wicked imitation of David Enthoven. 'Home James,' he says to his driver.

Rob's turnaround has lasted. He's still clean, happier in LA than he's been for a long time. He likes the anonymity, being away from the constant harassment of press and fans that he gets at home. In LA he can, by and large, do the normal things that normal people do. Like take his dogs for a walk without being pursued by paparazzi. Go to a movie or out for a meal with friends. 'He's able to live an ordinary life,' says manager Tim Clark, 'for the first time since he joined Take That. He can walk out the door, go down the street, not be hassled.' Everything's relative, of course. Two recent outings with current girlfriend Rachel Hunter have made the front of the *News of the World* (and pages 2, 3, 4 & 5). But still, by Rob's London standards, that's a quiet life.

When he talked about his future last year, Rob was worn out with touring and performing. He was intending to fulfil his commitments with the summer tour of the UK and Ireland and the autumn tour of the Far East and Australasia, then have that longed-for year off. But as it was Rob, forever contradictory and surprising, things didn't turn out as simply as even he had planned.

The story began in early 2001 when Rob was asked to sing the swing classic 'Have You Met Miss Jones?' for the soundtrack of the movie *Bridget Jones's Diary*. Screenwriter Richard Curtis and music supervisor Nick Angel reckoned Rob was the only performer they wanted, a contemporary Sinatra; and Rob was excited to take up the challenge. 'He sailed through it,' says Josie Cliff, 'loved it, said, "God, this is easy, we should make an album."' The idea developed momentum when Rob was in LA in May 2001, filming a short promotional video for the recording of 'We Are The Champions' for the soundtrack of *The Knight's Tale*.

Celebrated chat show host Jay Leno had got to hear that Rob was in town and invited him to sing 'Have You Met Miss Jones?' on his show (*Bridget Jones's Diary* was a huge hit in America at the time). Rob obliged and thoroughly enjoyed the experience. When he returned to London, he went straight in to meet managers Tim and David in the offices of IE Music.

'He just walked in here,' says David, 'and said, "Look guys, why don't we do a swing album for Christmas?"'

'We were,' says Tim, 'initially a little concerned, because we hadn't planned an album and Rob at that time was ubiquitous; we were trying to keep him out of the press, just give him the break he wanted. I think if he'd said, "I've written all these songs and I want to do a new Robbie album," we'd probably have said, "Look, wait a bit, there needs to be a bit of space, a bit of time."' But as this was completely different from anything Rob had done before, the managers agreed to go for it.

'And then,' laughs Tim, 'the fun and games began, because I think EMI believed that we were trying to pull a fast one to get out of Rob's contract.'

Rob had signed up with the record company for four albums. He'd produced three. EMI were unenthusiastic, wouldn't initially accept the proposed swing album as 'a commitment album'. 'The words they used,' says David, laughing at the way things turned out, 'were: "This is not going to be commercially commensurate."'

But Rob was adamant. It was something he wanted to do.

Before Rob could get to work, though, there were

his numerous existing commitments to fulfil. In late May, Rob, Jonathan Wilkes and the inner sanctum decamped to the South of France to make a short promotional film, *Rob By Nature*, for the release of the double-A side summer single 'Eternity'/'The Road to Mandalay'. This featured Rob as leader of a gang of bank robbers, all disguised in plastic Robbie masks. The cast of the film stayed at the stunning villa above the beach where the film was shot, which they renamed Casa Mandalay. Blonde Kiwi model Lisa Seiffert was Rob's co-star in the film. Contrary to reports in *OK Magazine*, there was no romance, though it was, entourage and crew agreed, really steamy on set. 'There was just a great vibe between them, they looked so great together,' says Josie Cliff. And making up and in his trailer, Rob only had one kind of music playing. Swing. He was singing it all the time, practising the tracks he wanted to use on his album.

Next were the long-planned gigs of the 'Weddings, Bar Mitzvahs, Stadiums' tour of England and Ireland. Speaking after his performance at the Roskilde Festival, a week before this started in Dublin, Rob let slip a clue about the autumn's plans. 'I'm really bored with Robbie,' he said. 'After November, I'm just going to kill him off. I'm everywhere. It must be really boring for people.'

His fans clearly didn't agree, packing out the stadia of Ireland and England for some of the biggest gigs Rob had done in his life, 70,000 people at each one.

He was joined for the first show in Dublin's Lansdowne Road by four dancers and a six-man brass section.

Please Don't Forget Me

'What a fucking leap of faith,' he cries, as, having had a final pre-show piss alarmingly close to some trailing electrical cables, he waits under the stage on the platform that will transport him up to face the Irish crowd. Franksy kisses his hand, security man Jonah hugs him, stage manager Gary releases the counterbalance, the dry-ice swirls around his feet, and he's gone, up into the cheers and screams.

'Show me love, Dublin!' he shouts, after 'Let Love Be Your Energy'. And they do. Later, he jokily reprises a snatch of Take That's 'Re-light My Fire'. 'I've still got it you know,' he shouts to laughter. 'It doesn't go away.' Towards the end of the gig, Mum Jan is called up on stage, where she stands smiling in the spotlight. After the show, star and band are whisked back to the Four Seasons Hotel in the sort of sirens-blaring, lights-flashing, high-speed police escort normally only accorded to visiting foreign presidents. None the less, one very eager front-row fan somehow manages to get to the hotel gates before them. 'The Bionic Stalker!' jokes drummer Chris.

A week later, up on stage at Cardiff's Millennium stadium, Rob asks everyone who has a camera to take a photo of him at the same time. The flashes light up the stadium like ten thousand shooting stars. Then he forgets the words to 'Eternity', the song which has reached number one in the charts two hours earlier. The smoke-breathing dragon that was on Josie's list back in Paris in February is finally made to work. 'My special Welsh dragon,' says Robbie, in his best Welsh accent. 'I think we'll call him Jones. Tom Jones.'

Next up is a rainy, muddy gig at The Bowl in Milton Keynes. Robbie tells a girl with her tits out to 'put 'em away, love, they're minging' and a hovering helicopter to eff off. Meanwhile, backstage, tour manager Franksy manages to get himself arrested by a security guard. 'He's shouting: "You can't come in, you can't come in!" and I'm going, "I'm the fucking tour manager, out the way." Then, as he gets me in a head lock with my arm up my back, I'm screaming at him, "This is the end of your career in the music business." He's saying, "You wait till the police get here, then we'll see who's in fucking charge." I'll never forget the look on his supervisor's face when he eventually turned up. This guy comes round the corner, sees one of his lieutenants with the tour manager – probably the most important person on site apart from the artist – in a head lock. *Oh no, not him, anybody but him.*'

A week later in Manchester, Rob delights the tabloids by sending out for a curry from Shimla Pinks, while staying at the exclusive Lowry Hotel, which boasts a Marco Pierre White restaurant.

'ROBBIE SNUBS MARCO,' run the headlines, but it's not true. 'We always have a curry in Manchester,' says Josie. 'This place was actually recommended by the hotel. But I do think they were quite bemused by it all.'

Up on stage the next night, the fun continues, as Robbie tells the crowd, 'I was in Take That. I've also been in a couple of the Spice Girls too. I'm not stopping until I get Posh.'

At last something real for the press to get their teeth into. All summer they've been getting it wrong. Shooting his film in the South of France, Rob was 'on holiday with pals', according to the *Sun*. Then he had a new girlfriend, 'sexy Girls @Play singer Rita Simmons', a young lady he actually spoke to for a couple of minutes one night at London's Eve Club. Meanwhile the *Daily Star* has run a story about Robbie buying a £300,000 penthouse apartment in San Antonio. Unfortunately for the confused hacks, it turned out to be another R. Williams who had put down the cash.

After the Manchester gig, band and crew have a party in the ready-made disco that the crew have constructed under the stage, which is complete with bar, flashing coloured lights and dancing poles. 'This is great,' the band tell the crew, 'we should do this every night.' 'We do,' the crew reply.

The final British concert is in Glasgow, the following week. Rob and the band stay in the lovely castle-like Cameron House Hotel, set in verdant parkland overlooking Loch Lomond. Rob is visited by his friend Johanna MacVicar, the leukaemia sufferer who came to the Paris gig. This time she turns up with her father, a registered nurse, who takes Rob's blood to go on the Bone Marrow register. Here is a bit of press everyone is pleased with, as Rob's good example will hopefully be followed by many others.

Up on stage at Hampden Park, Rob thanks the Scottish crowd for their contribution to his success. 'You told everyone how great the show was,' he says. 'That's why I'm able to stand here now in front of so many of you. I'm overwhelmed by emotion.' Then, as he finishes: 'That's it. I've had enough. I won't be touring for a long, long time. So what you saw here tonight was very special. I'm Robbie Williams. Please don't forget me.'

And after the gig, back at the hotel, there is finally a bit of good, old-fashioned rock 'n roll behaviour, as Rob, Jonathan, Chris and the security guards decide to chuck Rob's telly in the loch. Then they have a better idea: No, let's throw Guy's telly in the loch. Then they have an even better idea: Let's get Guy to throw his telly in the loch. So the Musical Director is called down from dinner to stand on the muddy pebbles at the loch's edge. After a little persuasion, he takes the TV. He's about to chuck it in, when he suddenly realises that a trick's being played on him. 'You've tied it round my leg or something,' he says, laughing nervously. 'No, no,' they reply, restraining themselves with difficulty. Guy bungs it in and it sinks with a splash. When he returns to his room he finds a notice where his TV should be. GONE FISHING, it reads.

It isn't quite the end of tour, though, as Rob returns to Germany for his absolutely final European gig in Cologne. And yes, for once the stories in the papers are true. Rob does rip off all his clothes on the dance floor at the after-gig party thrown by EMI in the beautiful Rheinterrassen club overlooking the glittering Rhine. He boogies all night with his four dancers, band and crew.

Back in England, as band and crew take a summer holiday, Rob moves out of the Chelsea pad he's been borrowing from Roger Taylor and into his splendid new house in London's Holland Park. And yes, as reported, it does have a 12-foot settee, and a tropical aquarium, and a turquoise glass staircase, and an elliptical limestone bath tub, and (eventually) the $250,000 platinum pool table that he bought in New York after a shop assistant took one look at the scruffy jeans-clad nobody and told him he couldn't afford it. But no, the house isn't (as reported) 'trashed by vandals' before Rob's moved in. Nor is there 'a housewarming party', where all the guests turn up in Robbie masks. That's just an evening where a couple of girl friends drop round, keen to keep anonymous from the ever-attentive paparazzi. (The masks were specially made for the *Rob By Nature* film, then Josie ordered another ten because Rob got so pissed off being hassled at airports that he took to carrying one round in his luggage. Not that this stops him being photographed. Snappers catch him wearing it both at the airport and outside his home, branding him 'off his rocker'.)

Spiritual Home

Rob doesn't stay in London for long. At last it's time to get his teeth into the swing album. Rob, Guy, arranger Steve Sidwell, David, Tim and the rest of the gang fly to the famous Capitol Studios in LA, used in their time by the legends of Swing: Dean Martin, Sammy Davis Jnr and the godfather himself, Frank Sinatra. Rob is now working with the cream of America's jazz musicians, including 84-year-old pianist Bill Miller, who once recorded with Sinatra. 'I'm singing my favourite songs with a full orchestra,' he says, smiling with disbelief at his own good fortune. 'And getting paid for it.'

Rob strides into the elegant, wood-lined studio in his latest trademark flat cap over LA shades, blue denim jacket and black T-shirt. 'Hello everyone,' he says to the gathered musicians. 'Let's start with something I can sing. Do they know "Angels"?'

During the rehearsal and recording, Rob's enthusiasm and excitement is visible. He hasn't been so happy, he jokes, since he first took ecstasy. At the end of one take, his face cracks with pleasure. 'Fuckin' 'ell,' he says into the voice-booth mic, then he pauses with an unfamiliar embarrassment, as if uncertain whether to use bad language in front of strangers in this revered place. 'Sorry,' he apologises, 'but that was fucken amazing. Fucken 'ell! Sorry guys. FUCKEN 'ELL!

'Sorry for shouting,' he says, as he walks back through to the studio. 'I've found my spiritual home.'

There is a loud collective laugh. 'All the musicians love him,' says David Enthoven, 'even though they didn't know him from Adam, half of them, to start with.'

'I'm so glad to hear a young person doing this old music,' comments veteran Swing percussionist Harold Jones (sometime drummer of the Count Basie orchestra), 'because there's a lot of great tunes that are just layin' in the dust – I wish him all the luck in the world, because the world needs to hear this music.'

Guy Chambers is producing the album. 'He's singing lower down his range,' he comments, 'and that's much more relaxed. He doesn't have to sing on top of an aggressive backing track. These songs aren't aggressive. They're cool. Sassy and slinky. But he's totally upped his game. I knew he would rise to the occasion, but he's excelled himself.'

At the piano, the pair jam around together, as of old. 'And then I go and spoil it all by saying somethin' stupid,' sings Rob, then breaks off into a primal sequence of grunts. *Geta-weah-now-wooh.*

'That's not right,' says Guy, dryly. 'It's "I love you." You don't say "I love you" like that.'

'Just thought we'd add a minor twist to it,' says Rob.

Back at the Sunset Marquis, out on the roof terrace looking over downtown LA, Rob muses on the album's chances. 'There probably will be a school of thought that will look down its nose at it. Just by the very nature of how showbiz it is. But I genuinely don't care. I love this. I had one of the happiest four hours of my life yesterday in the studio. I'd been thinking, Why did I get into this game in the first place? And it was just for those four hours.'

When Rob has gone back to Britain, the American musicians will be sufficiently impressed to contact the Sinatra Estate, suggesting the duet with Frank that will end up being the climax of the Albert Hall gig. 'It was down to those musicians that the Estate got in touch,' says David Enthoven. 'Nothing to do with us. It was the musicians who pushed it through, said, "Look, you've got to let Rob do a duet."'

Another duet, though, is now in the forefront of Rob's mind. According to at least one of the papers, Rob 'bombarded' Nicole Kidman with letters and e-mails because he was too shy to phone to ask her to work with him. In fact, he wrote to her, enclosing his phone number. 'Will you be Nancy to my Frank?' his note asked. 'I didn't negotiate,' Nicole says. 'I heard the song, and it's so sweet and funny, I did it! He asked. I said yes. I'm a terrible businesswoman.'

'It's going to be
the best album
I've ever done.

It's going to be
the one I've
always wanted.'

So the next morning Rob waits nervously in the studio for the Australian star. He runs up and down the stairs. He offers to make everyone tea. He picks at some sushi, then gets soy sauce down his white linen shirt. Later he admits: 'I was like, how am I going to get through this and not look like an idiot or try to lick her face.' 'Lick me?' laughs Nicole, when this is repeated to her. 'That's a first. Well, I've been licked by a man, but never had one specifically say he wanted to lick me.'

Licked or not, when Nicole finally shows up, in a tan suede Dolce and Gabbana coat lined with a leopard skin print, the pair click. Totally.

'All right, love?' asks Rob.

'No,' she says, with a wild giggle, 'I am *so* nervous.'

'Cup of tea?' offers Rob.

The recording is made in under an hour. 'Wow,' says Nicole. 'I wish *Moulin Rouge* could have been like this.'

Nicole finds him 'charming and funny'. Rob has had 'a real blast with her'. 'When she came into the studio,' he says, 'she was shy and nervous and it was nice to see that. It was like, "I'm not the only one."'

Mum, This is For You

Back in England three weeks later Rob's big night has finally arrived. Wob Roberts and the crew have got the Albert Hall ready in a record thirty-six hours. Rob has had a stormingly successful warm-up at Ronnie Scott's. Now he strolls up to the stage door in a cricket jumper with a dashing crimson and black stripe. Round the front a black tie audience of nearly four thousand, paying up to £200 a ticket (one man claims to have paid a tout £20,000 for his) disgorge from black taxis. TV crews and press strain to snap the attendant celebs. Nicole Kidman is here (though not singing), Bob Geldof, Roger Taylor, George Michael, Richard Curtis, Brian May and all, not forgetting Rob's mum Jan. 'It's a great opportunity to have a great family outing together,' she says modestly. Jonathan Wilkes's parents are with her. 'Are they?' says Rob backstage. He nods and grins, childhood memories flooding back. 'That's great.'

Rob is now ready in black lounge suit and glitter-striped black tie, his hair slicked down in a Fifties-style side parting. Tonight, his kissing of the photos of his heroes has extra meaning. It's been a long journey from his front room in Stoke-on-Trent to the star's dressing room in the Albert Hall. 'I'm a dog's mess,' he confides at first. 'I really can't do it. I'm just not up to it.' But when the cameras arrive, he perks up. 'I've got pre-match nerves,' he tells them. 'But if I'm on form I'll just knock 'em fucking dead. I battered 'em at Ronnie Scott's and I feel that that's going to happen this evening. The Albert Hall is about to get fucken battered.'

He strides down the back corridors with his usual posse of security and trusted companions, while out in the huge expectant hall, the layers of elegantly dressed punters are bathed in an eerie blue light. 'Welcome to the Royal Albert Hall,' says Rupert Everett. 'Tonight it is my privilege to introduce you to one of the greatest swingers of our age, Robbie Williams!'

Rob appears in the upper loop of the glittering, multi-lamplit R that complements the giant W on the other side of the stage. His eyes light up and his mouth turns down as he contemplates the crowd. Suddenly he's dancing, beckoning, grinning, all the familiar moves in a special swing slow motion. Then he's sliding down a precarious-looking golden pole and breaking the paper skins on six big kettle drums, before stepping down crimson-lit steps between eight dancers – formally clad in little grey hats, low-necked black satin blouses and swirling long diaphanous Dior skirts. 'Have you met Miss Jones?' he sings, and the show has begun.

Rob doesn't try to be Sinatra. The show is peppered with his own trademark gags, personal touches and strong language. 'I'd like to introduce you to somebody who, without me, none of him would be possible,' he says, gesturing at Steve Sidwell, brass-section member, album arranger and now conductor of this 58-piece orchestra. 'Mum, it's for you,' he says before 'Straighten Up and Fly Right', smiling sweetly down at Jan at one of the circular tables below. 'But while there's music and moonlight and love and romance,' he says a little later, 'let's get butt naked and all fucked up on drugs.'

And the critics, pens poised to shoot down Britain's No. 1 pop star at a moment of overweening hubris, generally love the tribute too. 'It could have been the most excruciating circus of karaoke of the decade,' says the *Daily Mail* the next morning. 'That it wasn't is a huge tribute to Robbie Williams's abundance of talent.'

The stage is set for the release of *Swing When You're Winning*. In the meantime, it's clearly time for another tabloid Robbie-fest. The hacks are not found wanting. The showbiz world is apparently 'buzzing with rumours of a romance' between Robbie and Nicole Kidman, reports the *Sun*. The 'Hollywood stunner' raced from an appearance on Parkinson to join 'hunky Robbie' for a five-hour tryst in her suite in the Dorchester. The next day the pair 'turned up the heat on their budding romance' (any doubt about the facts now banished from the fervent imagination of the journos) during the 'marathon' video shoot of the 'Somethin' Stupid' video. They were 'like a couple of lovestruck schoolkids', a conveniently anonymous 'source' is alleged to have said, 'throwing fake snowballs and playing with St Bernard dogs'.

No 1 Down Under

Whatever the truth of Rob's private life, there isn't any time for the raging celebrity love-match the tabloids yearn for, because the very next Sunday, the Robbie Williams tour of the Far East and Australasia begins ('Sing When You're Pacific Rimming' the itinerary is titled). For the first leg it's relaxed. 'Four shows in two weeks,' says Franksy. 'It's like a holiday tour really. Trying to get everyone off the beach to do a gig isn't easy.'

The opening show in Hong Kong goes brilliantly, but two days later in Singapore, Rob manages to fall foul of the authorities when his draw-string trousers rip and slip down to his knees during his performance. The police are not amused at this breaking of their strict laws of public behaviour. While backstage David Enthoven and Franksy are fending off angry gun-toting officers, Josie and costume mistress Flo race to wardrobe to fetch Rob a new pair. 'This is a ditty about stripping,' he jokes when, properly attired at last, he gets to 'Forever Texas'. 'I know you're not allowed to in this country, so we'll all try not to strip tonight.' There is loud laughter in the young crowd.

The party unwind in Phuket, Thailand, where they have three days off in a row, chilling on the beach, hiring a boat for a spectacular day trip out across the turquoise sea to view the island location used in the James Bond movie *Goldeneye*.

The Bangkok gig is a stormer, but landing in Taiwan the next day, Rob has a run-in with his old friends the paparazzi. As the band leave the plane, the press pack are waiting for him – not at the gate as usual, but airside. Rob decides to sprint to passport control, only realising when he gets there that Josie has his passport. The journalists crowd round him, then when he tells them to back off, they berate him for swearing at their country. 'No,' Rob explains, 'I'm not swearing at your country. I'm swearing at you.' After the gig at Taipei, the entourage leave the country early and return to Singapore.

Now it's on to Oz, where fewer people mind if you curse and show your arse. First stop is Perth, where Rob and the band stay in the Observation City, the skyscraper hotel Alan Bond built right out on the beach. Rob loves his penthouse suite, which seems unchanged from the Seventies, with its flowered mirror and wonderfully tacky bright colours.

There's a three-day break while the band acclimatise and get over their jet lag. Rob's band-and-crew footie team, in their blue strip with the 'Weddings, Bar Mitzvahs, Stadiums' legend on the front, takes on an Aussie team that includes former Western Australia state players. West Coast general manager Paul Tombides is impressed with Rob's skills. 'He was supreme,' he enthuses. 'He scored two hat-tricks, has a fantastic left foot, is incredibly fit and in a class of his own.' Good enough to play in the national league, the coach reckons.

After the gig at Perth's Entertainment Centre, Rob's private car is pulled over by police for breaking the car park speed limit of 8 kph. But as fans catch up and start to surround the vehicle, the police wisely let him go.

The tour pace has suddenly sped up. Now it's gig, day off, gig, day off. Two nights later Rob's in Adelaide, then Melbourne, where, shortly before the sell-out show a full-on Aussie journo quizzes him yet again about his sexuality. 'Look, I'm straight all right?' Rob replies. 'Fucking hell! Tell the world. Sorry everyone, I tried being gay but it just wasn't for me. If I could take a gay pill right now, I would. But I'm just not.'

In Sydney, Rob, band and crew take over an entire hotel, the hip Establishment in the central business district, just a stone's throw from the green lawns of the Botanic Gardens and the white sails of the Opera House. On show night, Rob nicks Fil's kilt to wear on stage. And the press are delighted by the revival of their favourite recent Robbie story, as Nicole Kidman, in flat cap and glasses, turns up to the gig and watches keenly from behind the sound desk. Her visit to the after-show party at the Establishment's Tank club and Rob's reciprocal trip to Nicole's mansion in Darling Point later that night gets the journo tongues wagging again. But what do they know?

Now it's on to New Zealand, where, as Franksy says, Rob is the biggest star *ever*. 'He's like the equivalent of Madonna and Princess Di rolled into one.' In four gigs – two in Christchurch, one in Wellington, one in Auckland – Rob plays to 110,000 fans. 'We've sold a record to everybody and the sheep,' laughs manager David.

As Rob returns to the UK, *Swing When You're Winning* is released, proving EMI's doubters wrong by becoming his fastest-selling album to date. By its second week it has gone platinum in Switzerland, Germany and Austria. Meanwhile, 'Somethin' Stupid' is high in the singles' charts.

As bookies William Hill offer odds of 16–1 that Robbie and Nicole will get married in the New Year, single, album and DVD top the Christmas charts. 'I'm chuffed to bits,' says Rob. 'It's a fantastic result.'

Sushi Days

After a short Christmas holiday skiing in Zermatt, it's time for Rob to finally embark on his year off. He isn't, as some sections of the press have reported, doing this because his managers have ordered him to; or because record bosses are concerned his health might suffer; or because he's been 'down and depressed despite his double Christmas Number Ones'; or 'to keep his cravings for alcohol and drugs under control'; or even or to 'stop him cracking up'. It's something he's wanted to do for ages, and entirely his own initiative.

Now Rob tries to keep out of the limelight, enjoying total down-time with old and new friends in LA. Yes, he goes to some self-help meetings, but, as manager David says, it's all very different from how it was in Europe last year. 'Much as the press like to say he's gone to LA to exorcise his demons,' he says, 'he

did that long before he got there. It's very different
from how he was when he was on tour last year. He
was in early recovery then. Now he's moved on.
Now he's going out as Robert and making friends
and not making friends and actually having time to
develop some life skills outside this fucking mad rock
and roll Robbie world he's been living in.'

Denied their regular fix of Robbie, the British
press have done their best to keep the story alive,
usually on the subject of his lovelife. As Josie points
out, he's not doing interviews, so when a rumour
emerges, the journalists ring IE Music wanting Rob's
comments. 'And it's like, there isn't a comment
because it's not true and even if there was a comment
and he is seeing someone we're not going to tell you
anyway.'

So in February 2002 Rob is alleged to have fallen
'head over heels' with 'Posh Spice lookalike' Alison
Gunn, a woman he has actually met twice. In April,
he's managed to find the time to have been 'secretly
dating for two months' movie publicist Victoria
Schweizer, a woman he's met once. (The picture of
the pair having lunch in LA featured in *Now*'s 17th
April issue was unfortunately of the wrong woman.)

As for the facts. Yes, he has eaten sushi with
Jonathan Wilkes at Sushiya on Sunset Boulevard. He
did fly to Edinburgh in March to support Jonathan
on his first night in *Godspell* at the Festival Theatre
(where he wore a black kilt suit). He did take the role
of priest and marry his friends Billy Morrison and

Jennifer Holliday in the gardens of the Sunset Marquis hotel. But this wasn't evidence of Rob 'cracking up'; just 'a bit of fun', with the added advantage that he was able to give the proceeds of the *Hello* shoot to the happy couple as a wedding present.

Rob hasn't fallen out with Guy Chambers over Will Young; this may well be because Guy has never worked with Will Young. Nor has Rob been given his own star on the Hollywood Walk of Fame; that honour was Ozzy Osbourne's, though Rob, in his capacity as friend of the legendary rocker, attended. Nor is Rob in talks to hire his own Falkland island to make his own movie.

He's just been relaxing in a pleasantly unnewsworthy way, in the house he's rented from Dan Ackroyd on Mulholland. 'Are we doing the American thing?' asks David Enthoven, as he cues up for his first Stateside game of pool with Rob, on the deep crimson pool table in the pine-panelled pool room. 'Play what we normally play,' says Rob.

Website designer and new friend Scott Ford drops round. 'Hello Scott Ford.' 'Hello Robert Peter Williams.' And here's Al Schmitt, who recorded and mixed *Swing When You're Winning*. 'It went so well, didn't it?' says Rob, hugging him.

'Yes, yes,' Al agrees.

'*Didn't* it? It set the standard for how much fun I want to have recording an album.'

'It doesn't get any better,' says Al.

'It doesn't, does it?' says Rob.

'It's not
weird, is it?

I want to
come in
as Heidi
tomorrow.'

Another day he heads off to the Egyptian movie theater for the American premiere of *Live at the Albert*. There's only the tiniest sprinkling of fans outside.

'Robbie Williams?' says Rob in a hick American accent to the lone (British) TV cameraman. 'No, I came to see *Ice Age*. Robbie Williams, *no*. I know *Robin* Williams. He was, like, in *Mork and Mindy*. I don't know if you've got that in England. I'm from Wisconsin. I'm out in LA for a couple of days. I don't know who Robbie Williams is, no. Will you stop bugging me?'

Someone tells Rob that Frank Sinatra's old house is for sale. He goes to check it out but isn't interested. 'It's just off Sunset Strip,' he says, 'so I went to have a look at it. Not that I was going to pay the price for the house. It's like $10 million or something. It's really nice, but the house is right next to the main strip. So you're in the garden and all you can hear is the traffic. Also, you walk in and they're playing his music. The first picture that greets you is him. And there's lots of memorabilia around and I'm thinking: that was put there, wasn't it?'

But soon Rob's found a place he does like, and he's totally blown away by it.

Today Rob's turned up to the studio in a full Superman outfit. He sits up at the mixing desk, swivelling back and forth in the black leather revolving chair, his eyes bright, plucking gently at his crimson gown, pulling hard at his nineteenth cigarette of the day, as he listens to the playback of the song he and the guys have just recorded.

Producer Steve Power approaches. 'What's it called?' he asks.

'What?' says Rob.

'That song?'

'What?' says Rob.

'What's it called? That song?'

'What?'

'Don't fucking piss about.' Steve squeezes his shoulder affectionately.

'It's called,' says Rob, lost in thought, 'Song Three.' His eyes brighten. 'Song Three. Shall we put down Song Three? Shall we do that, Dave?' He looks over at Enthoven, grinning broadly in the shadows. 'We've gotta, haven't we? Shall we do that? Song Three?'

So it's called Song Three.

Rob strokes the padded crimson chest of his Superman outfit. 'It's not weird, is it?' he says. 'It's just not weird. I want to come in as Heidi tomorrow.' He laughs and makes a gesture describing ringlets in his hair.

'Can we listen to "Feel" again?' he asks.

> Come and hold my hand
> I want to contact the living
> Not sure I understand
> This role I've been given

I sit and talk to God
And he just laughs at my plans
My head speaks a language
I don't understand

I just want to feel real love
In the home that I live in
'Cause I got too much life
Running through my veins
Going to waste

I don't want to die
But I ain't keen on living either
Before I fall in love
I'm preparing to leave her
I scare myself to death
That's why I keep on running
Before I've arrived
I can see myself coming

I just want to feel real love
In the home that I live in
There's a hole in my soul
Can't you see it in my face
Of real disgrace
I need to feel real love
And a life ever after
I feel like giving up

I just want to feel real love
In the home that I live in
I got too much love
Running through my veins
Going to waste

I just want to feel real love
In a life ever after
There's a hole in my soul
Can't you see it in my face
It's a real disgrace

Come and hold my hand
I want to contact the living
Not sure I understand
This role I've been given
Not sure I understand
Not sure I understand
Not sure I understand
Not sure I understand

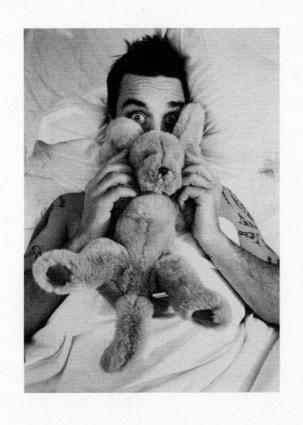

Enough